# Live Big, Dream Big, BE BIG!

## Building a Better You!

Dr. Jerry A. Grillo, Jr.

FZM Publishing
*"Live Big, Dream Big, BE BIG!"*
Copyright 2016
P.O. Box 3707
Hickory, NC. 28603
www.fogzonedesigns.com



All Scriptures, unless indicated, are taken from the King James Version.

Scripture quotations marked NKJV are taken from the New King James Version.

Scripture quotations marked NIV are taken from the New International Version.



Printed in the United States of America.

ISBN: 978-0-9977689-1-6

# TABLE OF CONTENT

# Foreword

It is my honor to highly recommend Bishop Grillo's newest book, "Build A Bigger Business By Building a Bigger You!"

I have been very blessed to make millions of dollars in the direct selling industry. The only way to truly manifest the life you desire in the external world is to change your internal world. Everything in your life currently is the direct result of previous thinking. Dr. Grillo has helped mentor me and my team for the last few years. As a result of his insight and wisdom, my team has elevated its leadership skills and ability to remove self-imposed limitations and unleash their full potential along with learning to walk in perpetual favor.

Many books and self-declared gurus are available today, but often it's just hype & propaganda. Dr. Grillo will give you the principles to help you live a remarkable life. His keys to abundant living and success are applicable to anyone desiring to walk away from mediocrity and live life without restraints. Dr. Grillo has a profound and effective way of unfolding the scriptures so you can see God's divine plan for you to live in increase. Your income will always rise to wherever you are in life; so in order to earn more, you must become more.

This book will provide you a blueprint on how to discipline your thought life and learn the skills to demand life to give you the very best. I have learned in my entrepreneurial journey that proven mentorship is more valuable than college degrees and decades of income. If you are a leader, I would suggest you get this book into the hands of everyone you are connected to. It will help accelerate their journey. It will stretch them to get out of their comfort zone. It will awaken the giant killer within them and allow them to be an elite warrior of faith and a business builder that is successful because you are now a people builder.

The ultra-successful do not succeed by accident. They master their mind and skillset. They are the architects of their destiny. You must learn before you can earn! From the time you start this book until you finish it, you will gain insight that will guarantee that you live a life of significance & complete fulfillment.

Kevin Mullens

Author, Mentor, Team builder, "7-figure per year earner" in the Direct Selling Industry

# Introduction

The average American makes $51,017.00 a year and is $225,238.00 in debt. As they say in poker, *"If you've been in the game for 30 minutes and don't know who the sucker is, you're the sucker."*

**You never want to be the sucker!**

Imagine if you could have the years back that you wasted dating the wrong person, get back the money you lost on bad investments, take back the lost decades you spent in the wrong career.

**You're Not Totally Free, Until Your Money is Free**

One of the greatest wishes every human has is to get back the wasted years of their life. Unfortunately, I can't help you regain wasted years. Actually, no one can, but I can help you stop wasting your present and move you into your preordained destiny.

I asked myself many years ago, **how bad do I want it? How bad do I want more?** What am I willing to do to get it? What am I willing to change? Who have I been listening to that hasn't changed me at all? What books do I need to read so I can find out what I need to know and where I need to go? Where do I succeed and what environments to I excel in? Who's voice do I trust to correct me? What would I be willing to walk away from so that I can walk on a different path? The truth is that half of your failure is probably attached to a person you've decided to hang with. Your first understanding of Networking is who you've chosen to be friends with. It's time you build a Network that will help you prosper. When you build the Network, you increase your Net worth.

As the self-made billionaire, *Warren Buffett,* says, "You only learn from mistakes. However, ***they do not have to be your mistakes***. It's a lot ***easier to learn from the mistakes of others***."

***Failure makes people ponder*** what happened or what went wrong. In the end, you gain an education when you fail.

***Success makes people party***. Reality check; people learn and grow more from failure than they do from success.

# CHAPTER ONE

# NETWORK DEFINED

There is no way you can ever build a life, much less a business, unless you understand that networking is an everyday event. Let me school you on something; you did not just join a business to build a network. You were born to network. The day you were old enough to interact with other people you started your network training. Life is about connecting. God built into His universe the power of unity. Really, that is all networking is; finding others who want to connect. Every person, every business requires partnership. If you have a product to sell, you are going to need to network with those who need that product.

***The whole universe works on networking***. Another term for "Network" is "connected energy." Have you ever heard that you are only four people away from knowing everyone on the earth? How can that be? Because we are all connected. You know someone, who knows someone, who knows someone, and that line can connect to everyone on the planet. We are all connected. You can use that understanding to network for increase through relationships. Then we connect to build teamwork.

**Laws For Financial Increase:**

1. Focus
2. Protocol
3. Networking

**NETWORKING DEFINED**:

A business network is a type of business social

network whose reason for existing is business-networking activity. There are several prominent business networking organizations that create models of business networking activity that, when followed, allow the businessperson to ***build new business relationships*** and ***generate business opportunities at the same time***. When we work our network properly, we are benefiting in two aspects:

1. We are able to build lasting relationships.
2. We are able to create a kinetic energy that builds financial opportunities.

Many business people contend that business networking is a more cost-effective method of generating **new business!** This is because business networking is a ***low-cost activity*** that involves more personal commitment than company money. The person is more important than the money is in building a network. Business that promotes people first will always find a future of being financially free.

Many businesses use networking as a key factor in their marketing plan. It helps to develop a strong feeling of trust between those involved and plays a big part in raising the profile and takings of a company.

Suppliers and businesses can be seen as networked businesses, and will tend to source the business and their suppliers through their existing relationships and those of the companies they work closely with. Networked businesses tend to ***be open***, ***random***, and ***supportive***, whereas those relying on hierarchical, traditional, managed approaches are closed, selective, and controlling.[1]

[1] *Thomas Power, businessman and chairman of Ecademy, an online business network, in 2009. (1)*

Networking has taken a bad rap through the years. The truth of the matter is that there have been more millionaires made through Networking Marketing businesses than any other businesses in history.

**WORDS MATTER:**

***Do not let what others say keep you imprisoned to a lifestyle of lack and loss***. The sky is the limit. You can do more, be more and have more. You can do this because you have decided to open the door of possibilities. You decided to dream again. You have opened the can of financially opportunities. ***Work hard. Work focused. Work with increase in mind.*** Do not let anyone or anything rob you and your family of the legacy that God has ordained for your future.

***Qualify the voices you allow to speak to you about your future.*** Words are seeds. Words are very powerful. In fact, words are more powerful than you have ever been taught. What you hear decides what you feel. Feelings are real to you. I know the old saying is that your feelings are not real, but the truth is even if what you feel is a lie, to you it is not. To you it is as real as it

***At the end of every feeling is NOTHING! At the end of every principle is a PROMISE!***

can be. You have to train your mind to know what is real and what is perceived. Feelings can create a world within the world of truth. I have seen the damage that feelings can do. I have witnessed good people ruin their marriages over wrong and damaged feelings. I have watched men give up their dreams because of feelings of fear. I have seen women walk away from right seasons because of wrong identity feelings. I have witnessed pastors lose their churches over feelings of offense.

***Feelings are great when they are in the right place.*** There is nothing like feeling loved. There is nothing like the feeling of warm joy as your family is experiencing vacations or holidays, or being surrounded by people who love you. You cannot live a healthy life, a joyous life or a saved life without feelings. I want to feel love as much as I have decided to walk in love. I desire to feel the presence of God, even though I am aware that God is everywhere. Feelings are necessary; but the problem exists when those feelings become tainted, damaged and now even control your decision-making.

What I am feeling may not be my reality. I must have a mind that is willing to live in the awareness of truth and not live in the mayhem of feelings.

Words create feelings or faith. You have to discern who is speaking to your now and who is speaking to your future. I want those around me who know how to speak to my future as much as they are speaking to my now. Words have to be monitored. What you say will decide what you feel. What you feel will decide what you do, and what you do will decide what you become. In truth, words can build your NETWORK and it will be words that will destroy your NETWORK.

One of the most common questions I get is, "What is the best investment I can make for my future?" Let me answer it this way. Warren Buffett made *sixty billion dollars as an investor* in many different types of industries, but he still says...

***"The most important investment you can make is in yourself."***

I do not care what others say about money. I believe God wants you to have wealth. I believe that God intended all of us to be financially free. His divine reality for all of us was blessings, but we as a people have made different choices and bad decisions that have altered God's divine reality for us. Now we living and experiencing an altered reality. It is my goal to mix the spirit and the mind to move you back into God's divine plan for your life.

I believe that this book is going to ***build a better you and in return, you will build a better and bigger business.***

Business is anything that you want to do that is fulfilling your divine calling and assignment on the earth. This can include investing in property, preaching the gospel, building a ministry, running a business, or building a Network Marketing corporation.

Get ready for INCREASE AND MORE!

# CHAPTER TWO

# BUILDING A POWERFUL NETWORK

*"What the mind can conceive and believe, and the heart desire, you can achieve."- Norman Vincent Peale*

*"When someone tells me "no," it doesn't mean I can't do it; it simply means I can't do it with them." - Karen E. Quinones Miller*

*"You take people as far as they will go, not as far as you would like them to go." - Jeanette Rankin*

Effective business networking is the linking together of individuals who, through trust and relationship building, become walking, talking advertisements for one another.[2]

1. **Networking is about being genuine and authentic.** If you think for one moment that networking is about a product, you will become very frustrated. Retail stores are about products. Dealerships sell products. Networking is about people. We are not selling a product, even though there are products in most networking businesses. ***Product is not the focus, people are!*** The focus is to persuade people to believe and buy into a ***lifestyle*** that they can do more…they can have more…and they can be more.

   You are not a sales person who is attempting to get someone to buy an item. *We are bigger than a product. We are advocating freedom.* You are a deliverer. You are moving people into a place where they can be their own bosses. Stop trying to be a vocal salesperson. Be a genuine conversationalist. Let people see your proof and not just hear about a product. Sell yourself. *Be confident*! Know within your own mind that you are helping someone become free! ***You are selling freedom my friend.***

   **We Are Selling Freedom!**

[2] *FOOTNOTE 2. Thomas Power* closed, *Sunzu The Art Of Business, 30 June 2009*

2. **Time date your dream.** Dreams are great, but dreams have no time dates on them. If you live your life with only a dream and have no goals or strategy, then you have decided to live in a fantasy that you will never achieve. "**Goals are time dated dreams.**"

***I am praying that you become a hostage to your dreams.*** Dreams are powerful weapons in your mind that free you from your present mundane life! If you want to survive any crisis in your present, build a dream so big that you cannot stop focusing on where you are going. Never discuss your pain, only your dreams. Never forget your enemy is anyone or anything that is robbing you from fulfilling your dreams. Become very protective of your dreams. Food for thought; everyone does not deserve to know your dreams. Qualify those you are telling your dreams too. Make sure that they are not sent to be a dream killer. Never share your dreams with those who do not know how to dream.

**Goals Are Time Dated Dreams!**

***Dreams are the focus of your mind that needs no boundaries or money.*** When you dream, DREAM BIG! Get a dream that is bigger than you, and God will get involved with your dreams. Get a vision so big that you cannot do it by yourself. This will require others to get involved with your vision.

3. **Your Power is in the PLAN.** I am under this persuasion. God does not anoint a man. He anoints a plan. You are going to have to become an unstoppable planner. Share that plan to everyone. Do not be intimidated by what others say. Do not allow what others are saying to stop you from what you

believe.

4. **P-L-A-N...**
   - Pray it out
   - Lay it out
   - Act it out
   - Navigate it to fruition

There is having a plan, then there is planning on presenting the plan. I understand that most first contacts are one on one encounters, but to be a high earner it is best to work through individuals to gather as many people as possible in a group and share the dream. The power of a group is greater than sharing with an individual. You have a higher connection rate when there is more than just one in a room.

***Become group focused.*** The atmosphere for inspiration grows swiftly when there are more in the meeting. ***Crowds create atmosphere.***

5. **Questions are the only boss that an answer will respond to.** Master asking questions. Questions are the acceleration switch to your future. Many fail because they have not learned how to ask questions. Do not enter a prospect's atmosphere ready to pounce like an eager tiger. Ask questions. Ask open-ended questions. Get the prospect's mind seeking for answers. Ask questions that have the 5-question seeking doors:
   1. Who
   2. What
   3. When
   4. Where
   5. How

Ask questions with these in mind, as opposed to those that can be answered with a simple yes or no. This form of questioning opens up the discussion and shows the listeners that you are interested in them and what they have to offer.

**FACTS ABOUT QUESTIONS:**

- A question is the only way to discover a fraud is in your environment.
- Until you ask a question your knowledge is accidental.
- Questions expose and confirm truth.
- Prayer is more powerful when you ask the right questions.
- Your questions dictate seasons.
- You're only qualified for what you pursue. A question reveals what you're pursuing.
- Not one of us is as smart as we think we are, so ask questions.
- What are the last three questions you've asked?

6. **Be a river, not a reservoir**. A river continuously flows. Most rivers flow into a larger body of water. Reservoirs are the opposite. Think of a pool. It just sits there waiting for someone to find it and get in it. It has to be constantly maintained. If you do not take care of a pool, the water becomes green and dirty. The same can happen to people. They become so caught up in their world that they forget that there is a bigger world around them. Become a person who is willing to help others.

   When you are known as a strong source of resource, people remember to turn to you for suggestions, ideas, names of others, etc. This keeps you alive in their minds when you leave their presence. If they do not join you then, they will after they have realized you were a source of resource for them.

7. Don't be **inflexible (dogmatic).** People run from dogmatic people. Do not make someone feel stupid or rejected because they do not see it your way. ***Remember people take time to change.*** You may be their door to a new future, but if they cannot see it then it does not matter what you see or say. Do not exit the conversation making the other person feel less. Leave and have something to leave with them that can help them see the truth.

**Change Takes Time!**

8. **Paint the picture of success!** Do not just tell me about it; ***paint it***! Make telling me so vivid that you are a Michelangelo with words. Use your words like color on a paintbrush. Masterfully arrange them so that I can see the bigger picture. Work at being colorful, animated and excited. Be able to express and animate what you want people to see. Labor to be interesting as much as you are being informative. ***Labor for accuracy.*** Nothing is worse than a person trying to show me something that they have not yet fully grasped.

***Words matter***. Words are doors, walls or bridges. Your speaking will either open a new season to me or close it. You will be a bridge to success or a wall to it. So make sure you are studied up on your ability to communicate your thoughts with precision and persuasion. Woo me! Seduce me! Show me what I can become and not what I am.

9. **When I change your mind, I have changed your world.** The word "selling" scares people. Selling is not a good word at all. What I want to teach you is much better. The word that I like is "***Promotion***." Again, remember you are not promoting a product, even though there are products for us to promote. What we are doing is much bigger; it is the idea, the ideology that you can be free. Not just free to earn more money but free to be and do what you desire. Free from earning a living! Free to start ***designing a life***. People are looking for doors to more. Many do not know that they can have more, be more and do more. You have to convince them to change their thinking. It is your job to raise their level of hope and expectations for bigger!

**Labor For Accuracy!**

10. **The Key to great success is FOLLOW UP!** Follow through swiftly and efficiently on all referrals you are given. The ability to do this increases your chances of growing faster. When someone gives you a referral, your actions are a reflection on him or her. Respect and honor that and your referrals will grow. You cannot grow your business with referrals.

11. **Do your homework!** This is called ***Due Diligence***! *Preparation is the separation between winning and losing.* I have a motto: The lack of preparation on your part, does not constitute and emergency on mine.

    - Prepared people are more confident.
    - Prepared people are more influential.

- Prepared people are better speakers.
- Prepared people are less likely to be nervous when called upon.
- Preparation is separation between the haves and the have-nots.

# CHAPTER THREE

# CONFIDENCE ATTRACTS PEOPLE

*"Believe you can and you're halfway there."- Theodore Roosevelt*

*"As soon as you trust yourself, you will know how to live." Johann Wolfgang von Goethe*

*"Reputation is what others think of us; character is what God knows of us. When you have spent what feels like eternity trying to repair a few moments of time that destroyed the view others once had of you, then you must ask yourself if you have the problem or is it really them? God doesn't make us try so hard, only enemies do."— Shannon L. Alder*

Networking Marketing is about people, not about product. To build a better business you have to build a better you. I know this statement is going to become a repetitive phrase by the time you finish this book.

- ***People are attracted to confidence.***
- ***Confidence is Power!***
- ***Confidence is the inner persuasion that you are the person for the job.***
- ***Confidence is the key to winning.***
- ***Ability without confidence is like being intelligent without a mind.***

**Confidence** is defined as *a belief in one's own abilities; a full trust; belief in the powers, trustworthiness, or reliability of a person or thing.* [3]

***Confidence is not arrogance.*** I have met arrogant people who were never confident, but I have never met confident people who are arrogant. Many believe that having an arrogant demeanor exudes confidence, but I assure you the opposite is what is happening. People are attracted to confidence but walk away from those who are arrogant. Most people are downright turned off by arrogance. Truly confident people show humility more than arrogance.

*"In Him (Jesus) and through faith in Him we may*

[3] *http://dictionary.reference.com/browse/confidence*

*approach God with **freedom and confidence.**" (Eph. 3:12)*

Two important words that sum up what I believe the purpose of Jesus was:

1. **Freedom**
2. **Confidence**

In my opinion, these two words come into meaning when we begin to become debt free and our finances become more than our needs. You are not really free until your money is free. Freedom produces confidence. Poverty, lack, and the enemy want to destroy our understanding of freedom and confidence in that freedom.

***Confidence decides position!***

There are two ways to being free. There is positional freedom and conditional freedom. Positional freedom is the most powerful freedom you can walk in. Confident people are positionally free, never conditionally free. There are so many who live in a conditional world. The only way they feel joy, peace or happiness is when the conditions around them promote it.

## CONDITIONAL FREEDOM

You have met these kinds of people. They live on a day-to-day scale. One day they are on a mountaintop high about life, their business and their relationships. The next day they are living in the valley blues. They move up and down the feeling scale without any reservations because they are connected to their *condition*. They are high on life when the conditions are high. They are low on life when the conditions around them are low. Their whole world is conditionally based. You will never build your business, nor will you ever have confidence living in this never-ending cycle. People will not stay connected to you, nor will they last in your business. Just so we are on the same page, the word condition means circumstances, disorders, situations, and the state of affairs around you that decide what a person is feeling. Conditional freedom is no freedom at all. It is a never-ending cycle of drama and feelings that create fear, frustrations and worries even in those who have decided to connect with you.

## POSITIONAL FREEDOM

Positional freedom is exactly that. You are not free by your condition; you are free by your position. The situation, the crisis or the storms do not decide your freedom. You maintain your posture and position above these events. Let me be truthful. No one is exempt from conditions. We all are subject to the world around us. Confident people have decided to live in their minds and not their condition. We are free because we say we are free not because someone or some situation has decided it for us.

I cannot - nor can you - control what is always going on around me. We cannot stop people from insulting us. We cannot hold back those who ignore us or are rude to us. No one can control how others choose to live around him or her. In reality, we are all living in a world that throws all kinds of situations at us daily. Too often I have gone to bed living a great and victorious day to wake up into a

**Don't Be The Fire; Reflect The Fire**

whirlwind of **crap** (excuse my language)! Like I said, "I can't always control what's happening around me, **BUT I CAN ALWAYS DECIDE WHAT'S HAPPENING IN ME!"** So can you! Confident people take control of their emotions. They tell themselves how they are going to act and react. They never let someone or something steal their power.

Someone once asked me, "How can you stay so excited about God for so long? How come you don't ever burn out?" My reply… *"I am not trying to be the fire; I am only reflecting the fire."* Let me be clear here. You will never truly be confident living life without Jesus in it. Your confidence will not exist in your abilities alone when you have God's son living in you, and you have decided to take up God's Word (bible) as your number one book for spiritual and financial growth. You will have an unstoppable persuasion that God is doing business through you.

***Confidence creates the willingness to fight.***

Those who lack confidence lack the passion to fight. You face your problems differently when you are confident. Confidence is that inner persuasion and thought that you are going to win. You cannot or will not be beaten. Confident people are focused on the game. They are focused on the task at hand. Confident leaders lead with pride, excellence and a sense of urgency. Confident people always win in the end. Want to know why? Confident people focus on winning. Winners focus on winning. Losers always focus on winners. There is a big difference in how you will enter and play the game. Confidence is a mental power.

**Winners Focus on Winning, Losers Focus on Winners!**

Confidence can be a self-fulfilling prophecy. Those with it may succeed because they have it rather than because of an innate ability, and those without it may fail or not even try because they lack it.

*"Optimism is the faith that leads to achievement. Nothing can be done without hope and confidence." Helen Keller*

**Confidence decides what you dream.**
When you have confidence - that inner persuasion that you cannot lose - you dream differently.

**Confidence can be trained!**
Becoming confident takes practice, calculated risk-taking, and changes in the way you think, says *Kay, Shipman, and Sincero.* Here are seven habits that confident people share:

1. ***They push themselves outside of their comfort zone.*** Nothing builds confidence like taking action, especially when the action involves risk and failure. Confident people start small and continue to take action until they become more comfortable with the risk. ***"Nerves are normal***—everyone has them," writes Kay and Shipman. *"The difference between a confident person and an unconfident person is simply that the confident person acts on their ambitions and desires and doesn't let the fear of failure stop them."*

2. ***They view failure as a way to build their information stream.*** Confident people are not immune to failure; instead of letting it stop them, they view it as an information-gathering session. "It's a notch in their belt and proof that they've

started moving in the direction they want to go." Failure is necessary! You are not worth anything if you have not attempted something that failed. Why should others follow you? Why should others trust you and get into your business if you cannot show them where you have failed and where you have gotten up and attempted to try again.

***"Confident people thank the experience for the lesson, and then they course-correct."*** *It is not the strongest species that survives; it is the one that is the most adaptable!*

3. ***They watch their language.*** Sincero says. *"Confident people don't speak badly about themselves. Instead, they question their self-doubts. Instead of believing something is 100% true—such as feeling like a loser—they realize that they bought into something that's not certain and they attach feelings to new belief."* Kay and Shipman call that getting rid of NATS (negative automatic thoughts): *"Women are particularly prone to NATS. We think we make one tiny mistake and we dwell on it for hours and hours ... and it kills our confidence," they write. To get rid of NATS, the co-authors suggest reminding yourself of three good things you did for every negative thought you have. Eventually this technique will help you eliminate the tendency to think badly about yourself.*

4. ***They take responsibility.*** Instead of feeling like a victim of their circumstances, confident people take ownership of their situation and do something about it, says Sincero. *"They don't*

*blame their parents or other; they take responsibility and change the things that are getting in the way of their goals,"* she says.

5. ***They seek out inspiration.*** Confident people read books, take classes, practice meditation and find coaches and mentors who have done the things they want to do. Confident people become lifetime learners. They are always seeking to do more in their lives, their business and their relationships.

6. ***They seek out mentors.*** *"If you're confident then you don't feel weird about showing your vulnerability and opening yourself up to learning from somebody else. Insecure people stay where they are because they're afraid of admitting their weaknesses."*

7. ***They have great manners and powerful posture.*** Your posture says a lot about you. Trust me! People see you before they hear you. Sitting up straight gives you a short-term confidence boost say Kay and Shipman. The co-authors suggest keeping your abs in and chin up, which they call "astonishingly simple yet woefully infrequent." Also, try nodding your head: *"You feel more confident as you talk when you do it—and you're sending a subconscious signal that makes others agree with you,"* they write.

**People See You Before They Hear You.**

# CHAPTER FOUR

# BIG DREAMS DECIDE BIG FUTURES

*"Don't dream according to what you can have or do; dream for those things you can't have or can't do." Dr. Jerry A. Grillo, Jr.*

*"Don't dream at the level of your income; dream at the level of God's unlimited power." Dr. Jerry A. Grillo, Jr.*

*"All of our dreams can come true, if we have the courage to pursue them." — Walt Disney Company*

One of the saddest things I have ever heard is the song from the movie, Les Miserables, "I Dreamed A Dream." While I was listening to that song, tears began to flow down my cheeks. I could feel the pain and frustration in that song. I have witnessed and felt this same pain and frustration throughout my life. I am not immune to the words of this song:

> ***I dreamed a dream*** *in time gone by,*
> *When hope was high and life worth living.*
> *I* ***dreamed*** *that love would never die.*
> *I dreamed that God would be forgiving. Then I was young and unafraid and* ***dreams were made*** *and used and wasted.*
>
> *There was no ransom to be paid,*
> *No song unsung, no wine untasted.*
> *But the tigers come at night,*
> *With their voices soft as thunder,*
> *As they tear your hopes apart*
> *As they turn your dreams to shame.... And still* ***I dream he'll come to me***
>
> *That we will live our lives together,*
> *But there are dreams that cannot be*
> *And there are storms we cannot weather! I had a* ***dream my life would be so different from this hell I'm living.***
> *So different now, from what it seems*
> *Now life has killed the dream* ***I dreamed****.*

When I heard this song, my heart just swelled in pain. I could see all the faces of those whose life has killed the dream. There are so many people who wake up every day, sit at a table drinking their coffee and eating breakfast with a death stare on their faces. Existing in a life they never dreamed they would be living in. The line that gets me is, *"I had a dream my life would be so different from this hell I'm living. So different now from what it seems, now life has killed the dream **I DREAMED**!"*

The truth is that no one will ever be or do anything without a dream. Dreams are important. Dreams keep hope alive. You cannot build a life, a business or a family without a dream. **Dreams create in our minds a powerful picture of limitless potential.**

I have heard many stories of those who were pushed into terrible situations. The one thing that kept them alive in those terrible situations was their dream. That dream that they hid in their hearts and kept in their minds protected them. I believe the ability to dream can keep you from buying into and living in your present crisis and situation.

**WHAT IS A DREAM**

Your mind is your personal world! The pictures you play in your mind daily are controlling your life. A dream is a photograph of what you can become, achieve, do or have.

**Never Trivialize Your Dream**

You decide your reaction to every dream picture your mind plays. You can believe it. You can grow it, feed it and protect it. You can decide to build your life around it or doubt and kill it. All of these actions are decided by your daily reaction to your mind picture, or dream.

God given dreams are the most powerful because they are mental prophecies God has hidden deep inside the psyche of your mind. There was man in the bible named Joseph. He had a God given dream. That dream swept him, like a mighty river current, from the pit to the palace. That dream caused Joseph to live through some terrible crisis and attacks. The same will be true for you and your dream. Your life, your business and your very existence of hope can live long and prosperous as long as you keep the dream alive.

Protect your dream from who is attacking it, no matter what. Be very selective and cautious whom you allow to speak to you about your dreams. Be focused over your dreams. Remember, a dream is a dream. You can dream as big as you want to.

YOUR DREAMS WILL BIRTH YOUR FUTURE:

***Never trivialize your dreams***. Never allow anyone to trivialize your dreams. Never trivialize someone else's dream. There are two types of dreams. There are night dreams. There are daydreams. Night dreams happen in the middle of the night while your body has shut down for rest. Your mind wakes up the inner sanctum of its subconscious and begins to play or replay a mental picture, desire, goal or wants. I have had some great night dreams, and I have experienced nightmares. Let me add a disclaimer for those who are not mature enough to know this. Not every night dream or daydream is a prophecy to your future. But God uses dreams. He always has. I believe that God

**God Will Use Dreams To Talk To You!**

uses dreams because that is the place where He has you where you can fly, swim, run and do the supernatural.

Daydreams are dreams we dream while we are conscious. Make sure that you control daydreams. They could also be the attack of the enemy to break your focus on your now. You may be learning precious information that will produce your future, and the enemy wants your mind to wander on a dream that is not meant for you to achieve but distract you from what you are learning now.

If you want your business to grow you must grow and see yourself bigger than your present. How do you know you have become bigger than your present? You start to feel the pressure and confinement of your present. That is the proof you have become bigger than your present. ***Decide to become so overqualified in your present that your future will enter your now and beg you to get into it.***

Look at where you are today. Then decide to dream at where you want to be in your future. Once you have gotten that dream, re-enter your present and make the proper adjustments to achieve that dream. Your dream will require a plan, change and strategy. You will have to make the adjustments if you desire to make it more than a dream and turn it into a reality.

***Unusual dreams will require an uncommon moment to fulfill it. An exceptional dream will require uncommon preparation.*** The most powerful thing that can happen to a dream is that you decide to take a specific plan of action to fulfill it. You can turn your dream into a reality when you decide to set goals to achieve that dream. Goals are time-dated dreams. Planning always produces *self-confidence.* ***Self Confidence*** is one of the keys to the unusual dreamer.

**DREAM WARNINGS:**

1. Do not wait for others to inspire you regarding your dreams. Motivate and inspire yourself! Look in the mirror every day and work on your dream confessions. You are your own cheerleader! ***"People are the future they are pursuing."*** You have heard it said, "Good things come to those who wait," but "Great things come to those who do something!" Kevin Mullens
2. Allow unexciting dreams of yesterday to die. Stop pursuing yesterday's life, goals or dreams. Let the past die. Do not feel obligated to keep trying to obtain them, especially if you no longer have a true passion for them. (***Isaiah 43:18-19***)
3. Do not assume that those closest to you are going to understand your dreams and goals.
4. Nobody can dream for you. Nobody can decide what you feel or are feeling. You must decide for yourself. Your focus decides your feelings.
5. Remember, different people have different goals and dreams. What is important to me may not be important to you.
6. Avoid intimate relationships with people who disrespect your dreams. I am not saying you cannot minister to them or eat dinner with them, but I am warning you not to become intimate with those who are not going to help you grow your dreams.

**Don't Build A Business, Build Your Dreams**

Dreams produce within us the desire to pursue! The proof of desire is pursuit. Dreams create within us the ability to move beyond our norm, our crisis and our present situations and enter a world that is magical and limitless.

Desire is the greatest seed you have. Just your willingness to purchase this book and read it is the proof of your desire.

**FACTS ABOUT DESIRE:**

- *Desire determines what you learn.*
- *Desire decides what you will pursue.*
- *Desire creates enormous energy.*
- *Desire produces endurance and strength.*
- *Desire is the force behind all change.*
- *Desire exposes those around you who are not connected to your future.*

**Keys To Unlocking Your Dreams**:

1. Decide what your dream really is!
2. Create within you the inspiration to pursue that dream.
3. Monitor and discern the right mentorship to help you achieve that dream.
4. Invest the time necessary to accomplish your dream.
5. Build a DREAM WALL.
6. Do not be afraid to believe for your dream.
7. Remember, God is wanting to help you accomplish that dream

Expect demonic distractions. ***Anything God loves… hell hates!***

A dream that is God sent will activate the enemies of God to show up. Do not be afraid to confront those who reveal they are not with you. Any uncontested enemy will flourish. Your business will attract warfare. Your willingness to grow yourself will attract warfare.

Your decision to have more, do more and be more will unlock the gates of hell to attack you and stop you. Why? Because if you heal yourself you will build your wealth stream. The power of wealth is influence. Your enemy is after your influence. Do not let **defeat**, **discouragement or distractions** stop you from staying the course and continuing to grow yourself. The bigger your dreams the bigger your business will be.

**Anything God Loves... Hell Hates!**

The enemy will never react to your past; he will always react to your future. That is why all warfare is over your seed. Your seed decides the harvest in your future. The mistakes you made in your past are already in the so-called bank of failure, regret and guilt. Your future has not happened yet. It is your potential! Do you want to know what potential is? Potential is not what you have done; it is what you have not done but can still do. It is not where you have been. It is where you have not been but can still go. Potential is not what you have gotten; it is what you have not gotten but can still have. I know faith is flooding through your veins right now.

Take time to build yourself in the presence of God. The better you know yourself, the better you can build your business. Take time to build your business on God's timetable.

I am 54 years old. I was sitting in my office a few months ago signing some building plans to build our first building on our 21 acres of land. I sat there all by myself and began to feel a little upset. I was excited that we signed the plans. I was also happy that we are moving forward. However, when I thought for a moment, I realized it had taken me twenty years to get to this first building...twenty years to build. I began to cry aloud to God. I said, *"God, I am 53 years old. It's taken me twenty years to get here."* I was feeling sorry for myself! Then I heard God's voice speak to me in my office, ***"SON! You're not in a race with anyone!"*** Our success is scheduled on God's timetable. ***Please do not forget that.***

***Do not build a business; build a DREAM.***
When God puts a dream in you, it will become something you can do, become and have.

***God uses visions and dreams to create.***
1. Focus
2. Progression
3. Expectation
4. Hope

**Without Dreams, We Reach Nothing.**
**Without Love, We Feel Nothing.**
**And Without God We Are NOTHING!**

***Dreams are powerful because they...***
1. Distinguish you from others. Dreams reveal your difference.
2. Reveal you.
3. Energize you.
4. Raise you. They keep your attitude focused for what is next.
5. Motivates you.

***Eight things I've learned about dreams:***

1. ***Your dream will require patience*** (Habakkuk 2:3). Waiting is not the absence of movement; it is the force that the future obeys. Waiting is not a

delay… it is simply preparation. Waiting is the season that the harvest is being created in.

2. ***A dream is often birthed through survived pain.***
3. ***A dream will require all of your faith.***
4. ***Your dream must be born within you.*** It must be your dream and not someone else's.
5. ***Your dream will require your focus and all of your passion.*** Passion is focused energy, enthusiasm and strength.
6. ***Your dream will reveal who belongs in your life and who does not.***
7. ***Do not be afraid to announce your dreams.*** Talk about them. This makes it very difficult to abort them.
8. ***Your dream will require persistence.*** Persistence means valuing your purpose enough not to quit. Persistence means you live according to your destiny and not your present situation or crisis.[4]

[4] *"The Uncommon Dream ISBN 10: 1-56394-601-7 / ISBN 13: 978-1563946011 / eB-135 Copyright © 2006 by MIKE MURDOCK*

# CHAPTER FIVE

# FRIENDS REVEAL YOUR OPINION OF YOU

*"If you choose bad companions, no one will believe that you are anything but bad yourself."*
*— Aesop, Aesop's Fables*

*"Remember, as there are people that can help you to roll the boat of your dreams, there are also people who can drill holes under that boat to make it sink."*
*— Israelmore Ayivor*

I know you have heard this more than once in your life, ***"Birds of a feather flock together."*** Your friends are the proof of the opinion you have of yourself! Sorry. Not trying to be mean spirited, but many people would probably be further along in their lives if they would just cut off some friends.

When the enemy wants to destroy you, He will put a person in your life to do it. You must become a qualifier of whom you give access to. Then you must know yourself so you will not attract wrong people in your life.

In thirty years of ministry, I have witnessed many falling short of their goals and dreams. I can tell you it was not what they wanted or desired. These people had the passion, drive and even had the knowledge to succeed and change. The one defining factor was they would not cut off their old friends. That one mistake has cost many to walk right back into their past.

Many have no idea how much the people around them can affect them. These are people who always speak about failure, their pains, their bad marriages, and the list goes on and on. Words matter. Words affect our thinking; they affect our atmosphere and can destroy your faith. Run as fast as you can from such people. Break connection from those who are not speaking about your future.

**Nine Effects Negative People Will Have On You. *They will...***

1. Demean your value.

2. Destroy the image of your future.
3. Mentally frustrate you!
4. Hinder your harvest!
5. Discredit your imagination!
6. Hate your abilities.
7. Debate your opinions!
8. Pollute your atmosphere.
9. Distract you from your passion.

***Stay away from negative people!***

People will receive you by your friends. I do not know if you have ever heard the story of the young lawyer and old lawyer. There was a young lawyer who moved into a new city, a small city that many would call a town. In that town, everyone knew each other. So this young lawyer set up his practice and hired a secretary. After a few months, he could not get any clients. He did everything he knew to do, but the people just would not call him. One day he met up with an old lawyer who had lived in that town and had practiced law there for over 30 years. That day the old lawyer asked him how was his new practice going. "*Not so good! I can't seem to get anyone to really hire me.*"

The old lawyer said, "I like you, and I want to help you. Let's do lunch tomorrow."

So the next day the young lawyer met the old lawyer for lunch. After lunch, the old lawyer said, "Let's walk back to your office."

**What You Connect To You Will Eventually Become!**

The young lawyer agreed, being a little confused. The old lawyer had not shared any mentorship on how to build his practice. After they arrived to the office, the young lawyer said, *"Sir, I appreciate lunch and the great conversations we've shared, but you said you were going to help me know how to build my practice here."*

The old lawyer said, *"I did!"*

*"How?"* replied the young lawyer.

*"By walking down the street with you and letting everyone see us at lunch together. Then by walking together back to your office,"* replied the old lawyer.

The next day the young lawyer's phone would not stop ringing!

What had happened? When the people saw the young lawyer hanging with the old lawyer, who had been practicing in that town for over 30 years, they immediately assumed that the young lawyer must be as good as the old lawyer.

Whom you attach yourself to matters. **Connection is power!**

- Access is a privilege.
- Connection is a qualifier.
- Partnership is a reward.
- Relationship is the result of Honor.

This is my motto! ***Discern swiftly whom you are connecting with and who is attempting to attach to you.***

There is a major difference between connection and attachment. If you do not learn these differences, you will find yourself in a relationship that is not advancing you but draining you completely.

Many times, I have mistaken the difference between the two, and I can tell you it has cost me dearly. ***Connection is my choice***. If I decide to connect with you, it is because I have qualified you to be placed in that position. However, attachment is not my choice; it is your choice! We must - as leaders, business people, and pastors - be very cautious how we allow people to stay around us. Be very focused on the people who are overly praising you. I have learned that those who are overly affirming me to my face are overly discrediting me behind my back. Here is something I have learned in thirty years of ministry. Not everyone who you think is against you is really against you. Not everyone who you think is for you is for you. ***The revealer is time!***

**Access Is Power**

**LOYALTY IS PROVEN THROUGH TIME.**

The Bible says that a three-fold cord cannot be easily broken. There is power in partnership. There is power in loyalty. When you find those who are loyal, they become the mortar - the concrete - in the wall of your success. There is power in agreement. Those who agree with our visions, our mentorship and our dreams are sources of encouragement and empowerment.

**QUALIFY THOSE YOU WANT TO CONNECT TO YOU.**

***Loyalty is a decision of the will, not an emotional response of the heart.***

People decide their loyalty. ***Loyalty is not an emotion***. You do not feel loyal; you decide to be loyal. It is a decision of the will. I believe it is a portrait of someone's character.

If loyalty is based on feelings, even Jesus himself may have become disloyal. I can tell you that in the role of having to serve a leader there will be times where your feelings and emotions are strained beyond comprehension. Good leaders can create bad moments at times. It is in that moment that you will begin to be deceived by the enemy. He will accomplish this by first having you start doubting your leader's intentions and focus. He wants to build a seed in your mind that in the end ruins your future and your leader's vision. Secondly, he will send wrong people to your life; people who are attracted to your leaking seeds of discontent with the leader you have chosen to follow. What causes this? You gave your discontentment away because you allowed your emotions to have a voice. In reality, you leaked when you should have been silent.

**You Can't Flourish Where You Haven't Been Planted**

When wrong people enter your life, they will have an opinion on what you should do. Their voice will be deceiving you with thoughts such as ***you are not appreciated... no one ever notices your effort and your willingness to serve... sees your greatness even if they do not... it is your time to lead not follow.***

You start developing the ***"what about me"*** syndrome when you begin to dwell on these thoughts. You start thinking, *this happens all the time...no one cares...no one loves me...no one notices me...* and the list goes on and on.

If you have not made the commitment to follow, the decision to be loyal, to remain, to stay faithful, to abide, you will most assuredly make the wrong decision. Now you will leave a place where God may have planned to bless you beyond measure.

***You cannot flourish where you have not been planted.***

*"They went out from us, but they were not of us; for if they had been of us, they would have continued with us; but they went out that they might be made manifest, that none of them were of us." 1 John 2:19 NKJV*

**"The Lack of Loyalty Is One of the Major Causes of Failure in Every Walk Of Life"**
***Napoleon Hill***

If they were of us, they would have continued with us. When they left, they proved they were not of us. I have spent many days crying over those who broke partnership with me before they were ready to lead.

We must die to human love, pick up, and carry the love of God in our hearts for all men to be loyal.

***"Hell has no weapon against a person who decides to love everybody."***

## Why is loyalty so important?

1. **Loyalty is the principal qualification for every person who desires to succeed in business, and in the body of Christ.** *"Let a man so consider us, as servants of Christ and stewards of the mysteries of God. Moreover it is required in stewards that one be found faithful. 1 Corinthians 4:1-2 NKJV*
2. **Loyalty will produce peace and security in your business.** Where there is no loyalty the atmosphere becomes agitated and aggressive. The rest of the church cannot find water to drink because sheep will not drink in an unsafe environment.
3. **For the love of God to flow there must be loyalty.**

*A new commandment I give to you, that you love one another; as I have loved you, that you also love one another. By this all will know that you are My disciples, if you have love for one another." John 13:34-35 NKJV*

4. **Loyalty is required to build a Big Network, a Big Business.**
5. **Loyalty is required to have a long, lasting and joyful life.**
6. **You must have loyalty in order to reap your full reward**. *"But you are those who have continued with Me in My trials. And I bestow upon you a kingdom, just as My Father bestowed one upon Me, that you may eat and drink at My table in My kingdom, and sit on thrones judging the twelve tribes of Israel." Luke 22:28-30 NKJV*

***Loyalty is staying in submission even after the agreement ends.*** When does submission begin? **Submission begins after agreement has ended**. This is the true test of loyalty; when you can stay connected when you really do not agree with what is happening around you. The family, our marriages and our businesses will grow and become healthier if we would just walk through the season of confusion and stay committed and loyal. Allow time for the plan to materialize.

***Loyalty is a decision of the mind, not an emotion of the heart.*** People decide to stay loyal. No one ever feels like staying loyal all the time. The same is true in churches, in friendship, in business and in marriage. Loyalty is a decision one makes. It is the persuasion that we are sticking together, no matter what!

What will destroy the church, your business, and family is when those around us become disloyal. They will begin to hang out with wrong people and allow others to talk down where they were once loyal and faithful.

**26 SIGNS OF DISLOYALTY:**

1. ***Poor Financial Habits:*** Laws decide financial increase. When someone is revealing bad financial habits, they are a prime suspect to become disloyal. If they cannot do right with their finances, they will not do right with those you place under them. Money usually reveals character flaws in people. The laws you obey decide your money and the laws you have disobeyed decide the lack of money.
2. ***Those who think they know more than the leader and could lead better.*** There are many who are smarter than I am under my leadership. When those under my leadership start believing that I cannot teach them or lead them, they will begin to break connection with me and start trying to connect others to them. Their attitude in meetings will show. In meetings, this mind set will always want to add something to what you are mentoring. Silence them immediately; trust me. You are the door to those who are connected to you.
3. ***Those who are not willing to be trained or retrained.*** They use phrases like, "I know…I know." or "I've been in business for years…" Those who come to your meetings without a notepad are not interested in what you know, but what you have.
4. ***Those who refuse to do menial jobs.*** Always watch out for people who say, *"That's not my job description."* Sometimes I leave trash sitting around in certain areas and watch to see which one of those connected to me pick it up. Those who do, care and

pick it up…those who step over may have a problem with serving others.

5. ***Those who are irritated and reactionary when you correct them.*** Correction decides connection. The quality of a leader will be in proportion to their ability to take correction. Move swiftly away from those under your leadership that will not allow you to correct them, and prepare to remove them from leadership. Watch out for those who are easily offended. The heart of offense can become a heart that is bitter and poisoned.
6. ***Someone who always gives excuses and justifies themselves in an error.***
7. ***A person who does not keep their promises.*** Do a credit check on all those you are bringing around you in leadership. If their credit score is terrible that could be a clue they are not good at keeping their promises. Of course, there are reasons for trouble. So find out why before you judge. Do background checks on everyone you are connecting with to help you build your business or ministry.
8. ***A person who is always lobbying for promotion and recognition.*** These kinds of people live life with a false expectation on how you should be treating them. They are consistently waiting for compliments and recognition over the smallest things they do. Their high expectation for compliments and recognition could be a severe sign they have a wound of rejection or insecurities. They will become a well of disappointment, not just for you, but disappointment in them. When false expectation or overly high expectation is placed on someone, the result is usually a season of disappointment. Deferred hope makes a heart sick. Deferred expectation causes the heart and the mind to become critical.

9. ***Someone who has never been criticized or corrected, such as amateur leaders or young leaders.*** This is not to say that young leaders cannot lead. It is to say that they are easily distracted. One reason is they have not really learned the mindset of loyalty. Take time to train young leaders.
10. ***Someone who is not attentive and taking notes or is uninvolved while teaching.*** Those who are connected to you will want to hear what you have to say. Any leader who sits under your teaching but appears to be disinterested is going to be a problem down the road. This attitude is a clue something is wrong in them. They may have picked up an offense or have listened to someone talk about you. Now they do not want to learn from you.
11. ***Someone who does not attend your meetings regularly.*** I hate inconsistency. I understand that sometimes meetings and gatherings have to be missed because of work, sickness or because someone is out of town. I watch for inconsistency in their attendance. Especially on special events or meetings, I listen for their reasons why they did not attend. I have witnessed in my own ministry the disloyal spirit that came from those who wanted to be a leader but would not make the meetings as others were asked to do.
12. ***Someone who poisons or tries to poison you about others.*** This one does not need much commentary. It is self-explanatory. If you allow a serpent to hang out in your leadership expect everyone to eventually be bitten and poisoned. These people will not sit silent. They will spew their poison on all who will listen. They are those who will not shut up. Trust me. The only way to deal with a snake is to kill it. By killing it, I mean asking them to leave.
13. ***A person who will not mingle and interact with***

***others.*** Loners have a problem, either with themselves or with those around them. Those who never mingle and interact with the group usually have internal damage. That damage will eventually leak. Demand your leaders to mingle to grow your business.

14. ***A person who always shifts the blame on others.*** Someone who cannot take correction is one thing but a person who always says their failure is the result of someone else really has a problem. Those who shift the blame are usually not teachable. The wound of rejection keeps them from facing their mistakes to fix them.
15. ***Someone who thinks you make too much money.*** If you have someone who believes like this, sow my newest book into his or her life.
16. ***A person who is not a team player.*** Team players are important. There is no room in your leadership for individuality.
17. ***Someone who is comfortable in your enemy's presence.*** If you are comfortable in my enemy's presence then you are probably in agreement to my enemy's opinion about me. I have a problem with those who call themselves my friend or leader and can sit in the presence of those who are attacking me.
18. ***Someone who never picks a side:*** Either you are on my side or you are not. In times of war, we cannot be divided. A house that is divided will fall.
19. ***Someone who trivializes your dreams and vision.***
20. ***Someone who believes you owe them something.*** These people will walk in resentment toward the leader. No matter what you do, you owe them. No matter what they do, you owe them.
21. ***A person who complains.*** If they will complain to you about someone, they will complain about you in

your absence. These kinds of people never see what they are doing only what others are not doing. Be cautious about allowing a complainer to hang out with you. God despises complainers.

22. ***A person who will not follow your instruction.*** Delayed obedience is disobedience. God does not bless anything that is in disobedience.
23. ***A person with a hidden agenda.*** No matter how hard someone serves you, they will eventually leave and usually leave wrong if they have a hidden agenda. These people are about one thing and one thing only, their agenda and their promotion.
24. ***A person who causes you frustration during and after great attacks.*** Those who cannot discern you have just come out of a season of attack are more concerned about their needs than the needs of the leader. Be very careful with those around you who cause you frustration. Frustration can create seasons of wrong decisions. In the end, these people will not stick with you when the waters in your business start getting rough. Frustration is a distraction. Frustration weakens your focus and robs your mind to believe.
25. ***Those who are jealous over someone else's promotions.*** Jealousy is the offspring of bitterness. Those who are jealous do not believe in themselves. They are wounded and focused on others and what they have instead on what they themselves could be.
26. ***A person who is consistently depressed and has no joy:*** Those who stay depressed are hard to reach. Those who are hard to reach will eventually become lost in the movement of the organization.

**THE POWER OF PARTNERSHIP**

Connection is very powerful! The Bible says a

three-fold cord is not easily broken. To build your business you are going to need people. There is no getting around it. You are going to need partners. Networking is all about partnership. There are keys to building powerful and unbreakable connection with others. You need to study these keys. I have discovered more than once that nice people are not always great people to connect to.

**"When Helping You Is Hurting Me, It's Time For Me To Stop Helping You."**

1. ***Continually evaluate the returns you receive from every investment you make into someone else.***

   Pouring into people is a great achievement. The danger of loving to help people is that the people you are helping to grow may not have the same passion as you do. You have to make sure that your time is reproducing success. When helping someone that is hurting you, it's time to stop helping.

   - Stop giving information to those who are not going to use it.
   - Stop counseling those who will not change.
   - Sometimes it is good to know that it was not what you had that is killing you but something you added.

2. ***Wrong people can create wrong consequences.*** Make the decision to connect with those who have great content not just great appearance. Try before you trust. Remember, someone you are trusting maybe trusting someone you would not. I have witnessed it so many times; people have to pay

terrible dividends for the friendships they made. Qualify everyone. You may need to cut some people off.

3. ***You will never know who belongs in your life until you know what and where you are going.*** Decide your destination and those who belong in your journey will appear. Those who are assigned to connect to you will connect to where you are going as much to who you are.
4. ***You have to know your assignment to know who is assigned to you.***

# CHAPTER SIX

# OBSTACLES TO YOUR SUCCESS

*"If you can't live through adversity, you'll never be good at what you do. You have to live through the unfair things... and keep your eyes focused on what you have to do."*
*— Maurice "Hank" Greenber*

*"All successes require warfare..." Dr. Jerry Grillo*

An obstacle is anything that is blocking you or hindering you from becoming all you can become.

An obstacle is anything that obstructs or hinders your progress.

It is important to understand that having abilities, being anointed, having great strength, or possessing great wealth does not stop you from having to face and overcome obstacles.

**Crisis Happens!**

We all want to be successful. I am under the persuasion that people genuinely want to be a success in their lives. Fathers desire to be successful fathers. Mothers desire to be successful mothers. Husbands and wives desire to be successful spouses and partners. Business people desire to succeed. Athletes desire to be the best on their team. I cannot imagine anyone entering a field to be a failure. Unfortunately, many people attempt to enter a field of achievement just to end up failing. What caused them to fail? They did not see or know how to overcome the obstacles that were set before them.

I have witnessed both sides in my line of work. Failure is the one I witness the most. Truthfully, most people do not enter my life until they have encountered a crisis that drove them to God or back to God. These people have usually given up on life, given up on believing and given up on trying again. They have chosen to stay in an impoverished place, ***but I do not believe***

***they were always like that.*** Somewhere they fell. Somewhere they experienced a defeat or a setback that cost them their willingness to dream and hope for change. This mindset in itself is an obstacle; the unwillingness to try, to get up and to even believe again. You must understand what success is and then discover what obstacles are attempting to keep you from succeeding if you want to build a bigger you.

**What is true success?**

***Is success determined by how much money you have?***

I know that money can buy many things. Money can give you some of the greatest liberties and options. Options you may never have had if you did not have the money to do it. Money can help you have a better vacation, buy you a bigger house, a better car, nicer clothes and so on.

Money cannot buy you a home. Money cannot buy you happiness. It may make a situation less stressful, but it can never give you real joy. Money cannot buy health or cure sickness. I read a comment one time by the billionaire, Sam Walton, founder of Wal-Mart. He was dying of cancer and at the end of his life he said, *"I would give up all the monies I've made... all the billions if I could just get my health back."*

So is that it? Is health where real success **is**? I have known people who had health but no money. ***They were miserable***.

It is not health! It is not money! What is real success? Success is when you know your purpose! Death is not the worst thing that could happen to a person; the worst thing is living a life with no purpose. Misery in life is being a ship without a rudder, a life without focus, a mind without successful thoughts.

**All Success Requires Warfare**

Everyone wants to succeed. No one I know sets goals to fail. People do not enter relationships to later get divorced or become enemies. We do not decide to take a trip, simply to get lost on our journey. **No one wants to fail**, but in reality, we all have experienced failure. Things have gotten in my way just like they have yours. Those things have slowed us down, and in some cases caused us to fail miserably. There are some specific things that are common obstacles in most all of my failures. These hindrances, these obstacles cause great defeats or at best slow us down so that we miss the appointment for our next season.

I can tell you this truth. There is no success without warfare. There is no joy, no peace, no anything in life that does not come without a fight. The real question in life is this. Are you willing to fight? What are you willing to do to have a great marriage, home, health and success? If you are not willing to go to war for it, you will not ever obtain it. I can promise you that! No, I am not prophesying to you. This is the cold inevitable fact.

Warfare begins when the enemy wants the same thing you want. An enemy is always attracted to those who want more. I do not understand it, but I can tell you this is the truth. Never under estimate your struggles. Struggles are a clue to what you are anointed to do. Warfare is attracted to the anointing. Warfare could be a sign you are going the right way.

**OBSTACLE ONE: Your own mindset!** *"For as he thinks in his heart, so is he..." Proverbs 23:7*

***Doubt kills everything!*** It kills confidence. It destroys faith. Doubt lays waste to hope and expectation. Doubt is so deadly it even kept Jesus from doing miracles in Nazareth. Another word for doubt is "unbelief." How you see yourself determines how others see you. You will never rise above your own self-image. When you have no self-value, you have no reason to be or do anything of value. I know this first hand. For years, I suffered from a low self-image. Failure is the only thing you live and experience when there is doubt in your own mind over your abilities. After a while, you will develop an attitude of 'why even raise my standards? All I ever do is fail anyway.'

Doubt will kill your dreams. Doubt will kill your relationships. Where there is no trust there is doubt. What is confidence? It is a mind that overcomes doubt. Confidence is the certainty of your assignment. *"Winners always want the ball when the game is on the line."* When you believe in yourself, you always want the ball or the assignment. You are the person in the crowd who is yelling 'pick me, pick me!'

**SELF TALK IGNITES YOUR CONFIDENCE**

People retain sixty percent of what they read, eighty percent of what they hear and ninety-five to one hundred percent of what they hear themselves say. Self-Talk! Learn to speak positive in your life. Learn to answer all negative voices you hear with the words of your mouth speaking the reversal. Positive words have power. Words build or

> **"If You Talk Like A Victim, You Give Everything Around You The Authority To Make You A Victim"**

destroy people. Words build or destroy faith! I was reading a book the other day while I was in a store by Pastor Joel Osteen, "The Power of I Am." Your life happens after the phrase **"I AM."** God taught this to Moses. Moses asked, "What do I say when they ask me who sent me?"

God replied, "Tell them **'I AM'** sent you. Whatever comes after **"I AM"** will happen to you. Pastor Osteen has a powerful list of **I AM's**. Put any word or sentence after **"I AM."** Here are the ones I remember.

- *I am blessed.*
- *I am healed, delivered.*
- *I am an overcomer.*
- *I am successful.*
- *I am a millionaire.*

You get it? Think about it. What are you actually doing? You are building confidence in your own self.

***Words do matter***. Words are the very thing that separates nations. Words are the thing that separates us from the animal kingdom. People have this power...the power to **SPEAK!** What are you saying about your life? What do you say when you are hurt? What comes out of your mouth the minute you sense an attack? Words are deciding your confidence. Your confidence is deciding you willingness to respond and win. Learn to speak victories every day. You give everything around you authority to make you a victim if you talk like a victim.

**OBSTACLE TWO: *Relationships...Wrong relationships are toxic!***

Right relationships can be so joyous. You create an environment of creativity, rest and fun when you find the right people to be around. Everything changes when you discover that you made a wrong connection. Do not allow the attitude of others to start messing with your environment for success and increase.

When God wants to bless you, he schedules right people to enter your atmosphere. When the enemy wants to curse you, he's going to schedule wrong people to enter your life. Relationships matter. I am not going to stay here long because I spent a whole chapter on friends. Let me say this. Monitor those around you who are showing the signs of disloyalty.

***"Someone you're trusting trusts someone you wouldn't."***

**OBSTACLE THREE:** ***Feeling envious of what others have!***

*__Envy is deadly__*. Your success could be in delay simply because those you have chosen to become jealous of; what someone else has. Envy is the door for disloyalty. Disloyalty is as deadly as envy.

> **"Envy is the pain and distress you feel over someone else's success!"**

What causes disloyalty? What cause people to rise up and attempt to destroy your success? I believe the number one root that produces the fruit of ***disloyalty is envy***!

Envy is when someone becomes discontented in where they are and what they have. They begin to build in them an inner feeling that they do not measure up. They start looking at what someone else has instead of doing what they need to do to grow, change and work their faith. When someone is not content with what they have, I can be assured they will not be content with what you have. Monitor those around you who are always judging others and what others have.

***Envy is the feeling of displeasure one gets that is produced by witnessing, or hearing of the advantage, or prosperity of someone else.*** The dictionary defines envy as "the painful or resentful awareness of an advantage enjoyed by another, joined with a desire to possess the same advantage." [5]

**FACTS ABOUT ENVY:**

1. *Envy will not be grateful for what it has.*
2. *Envy will not celebrate the success of others.*
3. *Envy is never secure in itself.*
4. *Envy will never stop comparing itself to what others have and do.*
5. *Envy cannot stop competing with those who have more and do more.*
6. *Envy will never be content because of its internal issues.*
7. *Envy stops the flow of worship in people.*
8. *Envy causes bitterness and un-forgiveness.*
9. *Envy is evil.*

**OBSTACLE FOUR: *Receiving "NO" when GOD says, "YES!"***

The norm is that when God says "Yes," everyone else around you says "No." Fight these negative voices. This becomes an obstacle when you believe that men, and not God, decide your future.

I have a great friend who pastors a very successful ministry in Tallahassee, Florida. His ministry runs into

[5] http://www.merriam-webster.com/dictionary/envy

the thousands. He told me that 38 banks turned him down for the loan needed to move into his present facility. People he loved began to discourage him from seeking out other banks. But he knew that God had said yes!
The 39th bank that he spoke to gave him the money needed to finish his project. Stay on course when God says yes. He is working it out.

**OBSTACLE FIVE: *Becoming disgusted where you have been entrusted.***

I know this subject very well. I was angry in the place where the Lord had planted me for years. I did not like the city. I did not want to be in Hickory, North Carolina. My struggles persisted for years. I even tried to move and start a church in the Charlotte area. I will never forget one evening, while I was sitting in a hotel room in Charlotte waiting to go down and preach, the spirit of the Lord said to my heart. ***"What are you doing here?"*** I replied, "About to go down and preach."

Once again, I heard this voice in my head. "***No, what are you doing here?***" My answer was the same. Then the Lord said. ***"I didn't send you here. I did not tell you to start a church here. Why are you here?"***

I replied, "Lord, I don't like where I am."

Here is what He said. "***Until you stop being disgusted where I have sent you, you have limited me in blessing you.***"

Disgusted means offended, repulsed, sickened, angry and discontent. You cannot succeed in a place you have allowed these attitudes to live in you. I have learned that you will rarely be led into a season you are fully qualified to be in or a place you will totally love. Why does God do this? He does it so that we will need Him; so that we will rely on Him to guide and comfort us. You are probably in the wrong place if where you are does not require God for you to succeed.

**THE BLESSING IS IN A PLACE**

Money is not following you; money is waiting on you. It is waiting in a place that the Lord has set it up to be released. Staying in a room and waiting on money to show up is insane. Money is not on the way. Money is not traveling on some journey to get to you. Work on moving yourself to the place where God has scheduled your blessing to be released. Your blessing is waiting on you to show up. It is in the people you are supposed to talk to. Your wealth is hidden in the idea you have been unwilling to pursue. "*Those who are planted in the house of the Lord shall flourish in the courts of our God.*" Psalm 92:13

You will experience the blessings of all four seasons in life when you are planted in the right place...

1. Winter
2. Spring
3. Summer
4. Fall

***Winter is soil preparation.*** It is in winter where the tree prepares it's self for spring's renewal.

***Spring is the time for seed sowing.*** In spring, we plow to plant.

***Summer... seed protection.*** It is the time where we protect our seeds.

***Fall***... It is **HARVEST TIME!**

**OBSTACLE SIX:** ***You stop sowing in a dry season.***

Many go through dry seasons. You are hindering your next season of reaping when you allow what you are going through to stop you from being a continuous giver in the end. You cannot reap in a season you have not sown for. You cannot call in what you have not sent out.

There is a story about a man name Isaac in Genesis 26. The Bible says there was a famine in the land. People were leaving and traveling to Egypt. God spoke to Isaac and told him not to leave the famine but to stay in the dry season. Isaac does something completely unnatural while he and his family are in this dry season. He sows seeds in that season.

***"Now Isaac sowed in that land and reaped in the same year a hundredfold. And the LORD blessed him." Genesis 26:12***

The natural tendency in a crisis is to withdraw, to hold what you have and to conserve your resources. This is exactly where you most likely will miss your opportunity to overcome the crisis. Do not be afraid to let go, to sow, to give in a dry season. You exercise your faith when you give. You are allowing your mind to see the bigger picture. You are telling the crisis that you are bigger than the problem.

**FAITH**

You must understand that laws, principles and rules, govern the universe we live in if you want to unlock a harvest in a dry season. The most powerful principle on this planet is faith. With it, I have seen the dead live and the blind see through faith. I have witnessed the sick healed and the lame walk through faith. You become an unstoppable force on your way to success with faith. Without it, you are nothing but a walking corpse, walking out your existence in a survival mode and waiting for your slow movement to end in a dark hole.

**"Faith Sees Past The Dry Season!"**

No one can build a big life without faith. Faith does not believe for something. Well actually, faith believes; but that is the weak side of faith. Unstoppable faith is when you do not just believe - YOU KNOW. The easiest part of faith is to believe that I can or that God can, but **to expect it** is faith in action. Faith sees past the ***dry season*** and into the season where the outpouring of your harvest of success will be manifested. Faith is so powerful that a person with faith has incredible hope. You give a desperate person the key to move past their present season and into a successful season when you give them hope. Do me a favor start believing in your future. Your future is bright. Your dreams are achievable. Your life is worth the investment of your faith. You are full of potential. You are full of dreams. You have not even scratched the surface of what God has ordained for your business, family and life.

# CHAPTER SEVEN

# FOCUS DECIDES FEELINGS

*"If you chase two rabbits, both will escape." Unknown*

*"Focus Creates Blindness." Mike Murdock*

*"The indispensable first step to getting the things you want out of life is this: decide what you want."*
*— Ben Stein*

*"If you don't like what you're feeling, then change your focus." Dr. Jerry A Grillo, Jr*

Understand the spiritual things of life.

Humans are divided into three parts. Let me make it simpler! Man is a Body, a Mind (soul) and a Spirit! Focus is the key to controlling the mind and the body. The body focuses only on pleasure. The mind focuses only on knowledge. The spirit is always focused on knowing the wisdom of God. We must train our mind to follow the spirit and the body will line up. The body will change when the mind is changed. Wisdom is greater than knowledge. The spirit always requires wisdom. What is wisdom? Knowing what to do and how to apply knowledge. All this is done by focus.

Focus creates blindness. When I am focused on my children, I am blind to my work. When I am focused on my work, I become blind to my children. This is why we must learn to prioritize our focus. For anything to be a success in your life, you are going to have to learn how to stay focused.

The opposite of focus is distraction. Distraction is your real enemy. Distraction can come as subtle as a small voice questioning your decision or focus. Failure's greatest ally is distraction. The greatest enemy to success is distraction. Success requires all of you. Focus is exactly that; it is giving all of you in a moment. Your moment is full of opportunities. One moment can change the course of your life forever. One right moment can accelerate you to your future. One wrong moment could send you backwards. Focus unlocks what is in a moment. Always be where

**"Always Be Where You Are."**

you are! I call it the "Be all in" mindset. "**Be all in**" your marriage and your marriage will succeed. **"Be all in"** losing weight and you will succeed. "**Be all in**" your business and your business will prosper. Some call this the LAW OF BUY IN! Focus is the ability to see what has been hiding in a moment. Just think about it. We miss so many things because we are not focused. The lack of focus is costly!

***Lack of Focus***

Ninety percent of people have identified lack of focus as their biggest obstacle to success. People who cannot take control of their focus end up spending their lives doing a lot of stuff but never completing and finishing those things. Focus is the key to success. Everything in your day and environment is warring over your focus. Your job requires focus. Your marriage, your relationships, your children, your health, your mind, your life, your pets and just about anything that is around you is trying to get your focus.

Many are confused as to why is seems that success evades them. What happens to those who cannot master their focus? They usually give up...quit! They develop an attitude of why even try to succeed because I am not going to obtain it! It is sad isn't it? So, what is the answer?

Another word for focus is **"Self-Discipline."** The Bible calls it **"Self-Control;"** the ability to exercise restraint or control over ones feelings, emotions, and reactions. [6]

Self-control is one of the fruits of the Spirit (Gal. 5:22, 23). There will be no success in anything you do

[6] http://www.merriam-webster.com/dictionary/self%E2%80%93control

without the power of self-discipline or self-control. The reason this is not a popular thought is that most view self-discipline as self-denial. Instead of taking up this mindset, view this as waiting and training for more...taking the time to grow you for bigger things.

Your respect of time will prove your ability to have self-discipline. If you are a person who is always late, you are a person who lacks focus. Focus requires discipline. Picture self-discipline as a type of selective training, creating new habits, thoughts, actions and speech toward a new and improved you!

1. ***Schedule small tasks for a given time of the day.*** Practice deliberate delaying. Schedule a particular task in the morning and once in the evening. The task should not take more than 15 minutes. Wait for the exact scheduled time. Start the task when the scheduled time is due. Stick to the schedule for at least two months.

   **Advantage**: *Scheduling helps you focus on your priorities. By focusing on starting tasks rather than completing them, you can avoid procrastination.*

2. ***Harness the power of routine:*** Instead of devoting a lot of hours one day, and none the other, and then a few on another day and so on, allocate a specific time period each day of the week for that task. When you do this, hold firm. Do not set a goal other than the time allocated. Simply set the habit of routine. Apply this to all you do, whether it be homework or projects, and you will be on your way to getting things done.

**Advantage:** *You are working on tasks in small increments, not all at once. You first develop a habit, and then the habit does the job for you.*

3. ***Use self-discipline to explore time management.*** Time management can become an overwhelming task. When you do not have control over your own self, how can you control your time? Begin with task-oriented self-discipline and build from there.

   **Advantage:** *As you control tasks, you build self-discipline. As you build self-discipline, you build time management. As you build time management, you build self-confidence.*

4. ***Maintain a self-discipline logbook:*** Record the start and end of times of the tasks. Review for feedback on your progress.

   **Advantage:** *The logbook can be a valuable tool to get a better picture over your activities in order to prioritize and realize what is important and not important on how you spend your time.* [7]

## HURRY IS THE ENEMY TO ACCURACY.

***When we lack focus, it is usually because we are in a hurry***. I know this problem all too well. I am so impatient. I always seem to be in a hurry. When I am on a trip, my mind can only think about arriving. Of course, you are asking, "Isn't that focus?"

---

[7] Keys to Self-Discipline: *(Time Management Series From Study Guides and Strategies.)*

It is but its wrong focus. When all you have is your destination in focus, you miss what's been hidden in the journey. Life is not a destination; life is a journey because when you arrive to life's destination your life is over! What have we missed on life's journey because we are in a hurry? Slow down my friends. Life is too short to miss what has been hidden in our day and our moments.

**"Hurry Is the Seed For Distraction."**

***When you are in a hurry, you make all kinds of mistakes.*** The seed for distraction is hurry. Think about how many things you have missed in life simply because you were in a hurry. The danger of focus is that you can be so focused on your future that you miss being focused in your present. What you are doing now is deciding what is going to happen next. Be calibrated; be focused and live in your now.

***Being in a hurry can create an atmosphere of stress and anxiety.*** I have been around people who are always in a hurry. I am always frustrated to travel with those who are in a hurry. Most of the time they are in a hurry because they do not plan their departure better. Therefore they are always pressed for time. That is not fun when you are flying because everything seems to be time sensitive at the airport. When I am in a hurry, I have noticed it makes my wife uncomfortable. My children act nervous. My staff seems skittish. Being in a hurry can cause stress on you and everyone around you. Hurry is the enemy to accuracy! I have learned this the hard way. Do not live life having to experience things

# CHAPTER EIGHT

# AVERAGE: SUCCESS'S WORST ENEMY

*"Keep your feet on the ground, but let your heart soar as high as it will. Refuse to be average..." Arthur Helps*

*"Good leadership consists of showing average people how to do the work of superior people." John D. Rockefeller*

*"To discover the thing you're brilliant at you first have to endure realizing all the things you're average at." Shane Koyczan*

Today, average seems to be the norm.

People are so unmotivated and uninspired. They just walk along life's sidewalk with a mundane stare of boredom. No one is trying to be extraordinary. People have stopped trying to do the unusual, the unexpected and the above normal. The sad thing about being ordinary is that ordinary people are never remembered after they have left the room. No one wants to follow ordinary. Average is an ugly word. I read a quote that really sums this up. *"Average. It was the worst, most disgusting word in the English Language. Nothing meaningful or worthwhile ever came from that word." Portia de Rossi*

Average! Here are some words that are kin to average; normal, regular, usual, typical, run of the mill, ordinary, mediocre and common. To build a bigger you, you are going to have to move away from common and average.

I am reading a book by Dr. John Maxwell "15 Laws of Growth." I love this!

Too many people are willing to settle for average in life. Is that bad? Read this description written by Edmund Gaudet, and then you decide.

*"Average" is what the failures claim to be when their family and friends ask them why they are not more successful.*

*"Average" is the top of the bottom, the best of the worst, the bottom of the top, the worst of the best.*

*"Average" means being the run of the mill, mediocre, insignificant and a nonentity.*

*Being "Average" is the lazy person's copout; it is lacking the guts to take a stand in life; it is living by default.*

*Being "average" is to take up space for no purpose; to take the trip through life, but never to pay the fare; to return no interest for God's investment in you.*

*Being "average is to pass one's life way with time, rather than to pass one's time way with life; it's to kill time, rather than to work it to death.*

*To be "average" is to be forgotten once you pass from this life. The successful are remembered for their contributions; the failures are remembered because they tried; but the "average," the silent majority, is just forgotten.*

*To be "average is to commit the greatest crime one can against one's self, humanity, and one's God. The saddest epitaph is this: "Here lies Mr. And Ms. Average- here lies the remains of what might have been, except for their belief that they were only "**average.**"* [8]

Common people can never do uncommon things unless they understand that inside of them is the potential to do more, be more, have more and grow more.

- **How big do you want to live?**
- **How big are your dreams?**

---

[8] *"The 15 Invaluable Laws of Growth" By Dr. John Maxwell pg 328- 330*

- **How much to you really want?**
- **What are you willing to do to build yourself?**

***God's gift to you is potential*; *your gift to God is to develop it.*** Your responsibility to God and to your family and friends is to develop and build your potential. I believe every person on planet earth is full of potential. What is potential? It is that inner gifting, that supernatural calling. Some call it the anointing; others call it that which God has placed in you that makes you different.

**"God's Gift, Potential! Your Responsibility, Develop And Grow it!"**

**POTENTIAL**

- *Potential is not what I have. It is what I do not have, but I can still have!*
- *Potential is not where I have been. It is where I have not been, but can still go!*
- *Potential is not what you have done. It is what you have not done, but can still do!*

Potential is hidden within you like gold hidden in the ground. The only way to find it is be willing to dig through all the waste and dirt. The time spent doing this will cause you to find the gold of potential. One ounce of potential is worth a whole lot of dirt. Hidden in your problem, hidden in your darkness and somewhere in your pain, God has hidden your potential. All you need to do is stop talking and worrying about what you are going through and start digging through your faith. Your power, healing and blessing is hidden in your potential.

I believe that when we were born, hell knew what was assigned to us and spent the best years of our lives pressing us and attempting to abort what God hid in us. The grace and wisdom of God uses that pain, trouble and storms to make us and unlock what He hid in us to be. The storm that Hell sent to break you, will actually be the storm that God will use to make you. Can you believe that right now?

> **"If You Plan On Being Anything Less Than You Are Capable Of Being, You Will Probably Be Unhappy All the Days Of Your Life." Abraham Maslow**

Build your inner man. Build your mind to see the power of your hidden potential. You were not born to be average. You were born to be GREAT!

## FIGHT THE STATUS QUO SYNDROME

Most people are naturally tempted to settle into a comfort zone where they choose comfort over potential. They settle for familiarity. The same habits, patterns and daily routine become so comfortable that if anyone or anything attempts to change that, they are furious and offended. Comfort zone living might feel safe, but it will lead to spiritual and financial death.

What will it take to push past average?

1. ***Hating where you are now.*** Until you hate where you are, you will never look for a way out. Change will never happen until you are uncomfortable with average.

2. ***Face reality and stop lying to yourself.*** People seem to believe the lie that everything is okay. If you are not where you are called to be, then guess what? It is not where you are called to be!
3. ***You must walk in incredible courage.*** It is going to take courage to walk away from normal. To walk away from years of mediocrity, you will have to decide to walk in powerful faith and courage.
4. ***Cut off all ties to your world of normal.*** Begin to do the uncommon. Begin to do everything with a mind of excellence.
5. ***Silence all voices that are not speaking to your faith.*** You need your faith to be intact. Do not let others opinions become yours.
6. ***Pray daily for the Holy Spirit to give you success and wisdom.*** You have been given the Holy Spirit as a gift from God. Start to use that gift. He is in your life to guide you, comfort you and train you for success.
7. ***Ask God to do business through you.***

# CHAPTER NINE

# RULES TO FINANCIAL GROWTH

**Five Groups of People:**

1. Very poor
2. Poor
3. Middle class
4. Rich
5. Very Rich (Wealthy)

Let's break down these five groups:

1. Below average
2. Average
3. Extraordinary
4. Great
5. Best

I was listening to a very wealthy mentor the other night, Dr. Michael Chitwood, teaching on this very subject.

1. The very poor live from day to day.
2. The poor live week to week
3. The middle class live from month to month
4. The rich live from year to year
5. The wealthy live from decade to decade!

***Wealth isn't reserved for a select few…***
***Wealth doesn't happen randomly…***
***God wants all of us wealthy.***

Now, before you get offended with that last statement, think about it. I did not say all of us would be wealthy. I am saying that we could be. If God is a good God, and He is, wouldn't He want all of His children to walk in wealth? Of course He would. I am a father of two children. I have always desired for both of my children to be financially free. I have always desired for them to rise to the top of whatever they are doing. I provided them the means on which they could. If they did not, it had nothing to do with me as the father but with them as the ones making the choices for their lives.

Those who become successful and wealthy have learned how to use what they have to their advantage. They do this by following certain laws and principles. Remember, the universe is made up of laws, principles and rules. These laws have been passed down through the ages of time. As a result, they are able to accumulate wealth and enjoy the financial freedom. Not so with the unsuccessful. Those who tend to remain poor despite having many opportunities to change their life do not follow the same laws that the successful follow.

In fact, in the majority of cases, the exact opposite laws are followed producing the exact opposite results. We must understand that every positive law has its counterpart. Doing the opposite creates the negative. So instead of building wealth, those individuals tend to decrease their wealth and become slaves to debts that they can never afford to repay. This is a curse. This is a tragedy that we want to cure.

**TRUTH**

When it comes to money, you really have only two options. Either you follow the right laws to make it, grow it and use it, or you follow the wrong laws and lose it. There is no middle ground. Sorry, I wish I could tell you otherwise. There are three rules and about twenty laws pertaining to this...

**THREE MAJOR RULES OF WEALTH:**

1. ***You have to take the*** **"Initiative."** Nothing will ever happen if you do not take the initiative. Anything

uncontested will flourish. So many sit in their boring, self-existing life, clocking time to the graveyard. All they need to do is get up and get started. Promotion comes disguised. It will look like something you were not expecting. It will appear to be a problem, but in that problem, the universe has hidden its opportunity. All you need to do now is take the initiative. Eighty percent of people in life hate where they are in life, hate where they work and hate that they have become lazy and overweight. Here is the problem; all they do is nothing but hate it. They talk about how much they hate where they are, but they never take the initiative to do something about it. If you want more in life, then do something about it.

What does initiative mean? It means, **"GET UP"** and- "GET STARTED." You will never lose weight until you get up and start to do something about being overweight. You will never win a race if you do not sign up and start running. Wishing for success will never attract success. Success is not attracted to want, wish or desire; it is attracted to those who are not afraid to try. Remember the old saying, "Better to die trying than to not try at all?" This is exactly what is wrong with society. People are waiting for a wealth star to fall from the sky and land in their front yard. It is not falling! It is waiting on you to get up and chase it. Your credibility depends on your success. People do not follow failures; they follow success.

The network marketing business is what I call the gospel business pattern for success. You have to get out and reach people to succeed in networking. You are going to have to take the initiative. People are not coming to you. So what! You go to them. Your financial freedom is connected to your willingness to take the initiative. Those who are willing to try will eventually succeed, and those who will not try will fail. It is that simple.

2. ***You have to be willing to* "Sacrifice."** *You will never have anything of value until you know the one thing that decides all things.* So what is this one thing…this one word? It is **SACRIFICE.** I believe this is one of the most powerful words in the world. You cannot have anything unless you are willing to sacrifice something for it.

   *Some call it the law of exchange.* Others call it the law of sowing and reaping. The world calls it a tradeoff. All of those are summed up in one word; "**SACRIFICE**." You cannot love without it because love requires a sacrifice. Why do we preach a gospel of salvation? Jesus was willing to sacrifice his life for ours.

   What are you willing to sacrifice to increase what you have? Will you sacrifice time now for something you desire for tomorrow?

   Think of any word that you think is important, and I promise you it will not happen without "sacrifice." Look at the word love. Love is proven through sacrifice. The only way a marriage will work is through sacrifice. If you desire a harvest, you will have to sacrifice the seed. If you want money, you have to trade your time for it. That is a sacrifice. The law of "Give up." What are you willing to give up today for something bigger tomorrow. So we have three rules for wealth. Get Up, Give Up…

3. **"Maturity"** This is the one we must all work the hardest on. Growing up! What are you doing that is maturing your thinking? Your desires? Your health?

Natural growth is automatic. When we were children, we could not stop growing up. Aging is an unstoppable process. Maturity is not automatic. You must be intentional to grow your mind. You must have a game plan to grow your thinking. If you really desire a better financial life, you are going to have to change your thinking. Increase your thinking and you can increase your living. This I can promise.

**"Increase Your Thinking; You Will Increase Your Living."**

The Bible says so much about success and wealth. Sadly, only a few want to embrace it. If you just took a chapter a day out of the book of Proverbs, you would see significant mental and financial growth in your life. There are 31 chapters in Proverbs. Decide to read a chapter a day; monitor what happens in your life by doing so. I promise that you will not be disappointed.

# CHAPTER TEN

# LAWS
# TO
# FINANCIAL
# FREEDOM

Laws govern the whole universe. There are higher laws and lesser laws that are set up for order to exist on the earth. I do not know your persuasion of whom you believe or what you believe runs the universe, but I believe in a supreme being. God is the originator and creator of all living things. God has set laws up over this universe. Those laws run the entire universe. Each law has been given commands to obey higher laws. For instance, we all know about the law of gravity. We understand that the reason everything around us is not floating is because of the law of gravity, even though we cannot see it.

At times, I want to leave Hickory, North Carolina and go to another state. I drive to Charlotte Douglas Airport and hop on an airplane. The airplane begins to lift off the runway and fly. What is happening? The law of gravity had to submit to a higher law. That higher law is called aerodynamics. Thus, a lesser law always submits to a higher law.

In business, there are business laws. When it comes to wealth, there are wealth laws. Here are some wealth laws to build on.

1. ***The Law of Cause and Effect:***
   The law of cause and effect states that everything happens for a reason because there is a cause for every effect. To make this applicable, rich people are rich because they do things that make them rich. Poor people are poor because

**"What You Believe Really Matters."**

they do things that make or keep them poor. The wealthy think different thus they act differently. This is the law of cause and effect. There is either a positive or a negative outcome for everything that you do which comes as a direct result of the actions that you make.

This law does not only apply to your personal finances, but also to every other aspect of your life. What you are experiencing today is in direct connection to what you decided to do yesterday. If you spend time to become better at what you do, then the law of cause and effect dictates that your skills or knowledge will improve in proportion to the amount of hours that you have invested bettering yourself. The same is true if you decide not to spend or invest time in bettering yourself but in watching television or playing a video game. ***Decisions decide!*** Get this law deep down in your mind. You are living the life of your choices. Decisions decide anything you are experiencing. My friend, Kevin Mullens, has written a powerful book on decisions. Everything in your life is based on the law of cause and effect. Stop blaming others or circumstances for your failures and start facing the cold facts. If we fail most of the time, it was something we did to cause it.

Financial success is simply an effect that comes as a result of taking certain and proper actions. To become wealthy, you must learn to identify the actions that will bring more money into your life, your business, your ministry and keep on repeating those actions until you achieve a level of a desired wealth that satisfies you.

2. ***The Law Of Faith***:
   This is the law of your persuasion, the law of what you believe. This law states that whatever you believe in, with feeling, ultimately becomes the reality in which you will live. This law also states that you always act in a way that is consistent to what you believe, especially, what you believe about yourself. You will never outperform what you believe. You will never go further in life than you believe you can go.

   **"Faith Is A Filter System To What You Can Truly Have or Be."**

   What do you really believe about money? The beliefs you have about money act like filters in your brain. They allow you to see what you believe in and hide from you the things that you do not believe. This in turn influences what actions you take, what jobs you will pursue, and the amount of money that you are likely to make. Another law applies here, the *Law of Awareness*. Your mind will only make you aware of what you believe is possible or real. You will have to stretch and change your faith to become a millionaire

   What are you willing to believe? If you believe that you are always going to have to slave at some boring job the rest of your life then guess what? You will. When you cannot stretch your faith to believe for something bigger you are more likely to limit your actions in a way that keeps you in struggle and financial lack the rest of your life. Suppose that you begin to believe that one day you will earn a higher income. What do you think will happen? Now that you are no longer limited by doubt and lack you are more likely to accomplish what you believe is now achievable. Everything around you changes when you change your belief system. What you read changes. What you spend changes. How you talk changes.

***Never underestimate faith***. What do you believe about money and your current and future financial situation? Positive beliefs are needed to become wealthy. Doubt kills and limits faith and will keep you living a limited and dull life.

**"The Rich Have Large Libraries; The Poor Have Larae TV's."**

3. ***The Law Of Expectation:***

This law is directly connected to the previous law of faith. Expectation gives energy to your faith; without it your faith is sitting alone and has no energy to reach or hope for better or more. The law of expectation is the law that whatever you expect to happen in your life eventually becomes your own self-fulfilling prophecy. This means that you are always acting as your own fortune-teller by the way that you think and talk about how things are going to turn out. When you expect good things to happen to you, they usually do. When you expect bad things to happen to you, bad things usually happen.

When it comes to money, wealthy people expect to live lives of financial abundance and have their net worth increase year after year. It does not matter where they are in life. They can be in great travail or battle, but they are always speaking in the mind of expectation when you talk to them. They expect to survive and increase in their future.

The beauty about this law is that your expectations are largely under your control. This means that you can decide whether you expect to be poor or whether you expect to be prosperous.

***If you can imagine it, you can achieve it.*** In Genesis 11:6, God himself makes a bold statement about man. *"And the Lord said, "Indeed the people are one and they all have one language, and this is what they begin to do; now nothing **that they propose** (imagine) to do will be withheld from them."*

***Your expectation is power:*** Your expectation about money is determined and limited by your own imagination. Wealthy people have a clear idea of what they want and expect to get it. Unsuccessful people, however, generally have the very opposite mindset. They limit their imagination. They speak so negative that there is no energy for faith to build a plan and strategy for better.

***If you desire financial abundance, you are going to have to think BIG!*** You are going to have to believe and expect the best in every situation. What you expect to happen will largely determine the type of things that you try to achieve.

***The heavens move at the level of your expectation***. High expectation is so important if you want to become financially free. As a matter of fact, if you desire anything you will have to work the law of expectation. As long as you think that something is not possible for you, you will never try your hardest to achieve it. I have a friend that is financially blessed. He named his boat, "Anything is Possible." I love this because in life "anything is possible" when you have high expectation and faith. The higher your expectations are the greater level of wealth you are more likely to pursue.

Having high expectations is not enough. Those who only dream of things, but are unwilling to take action and work hard to achieve it, will turn their expectation and dreams into a fantasy.

4. ***The Law Of Attraction:***

This law gets a lot of attack from church folks. I really do not see why. This law states that you attract into your life the people, circumstances and events that are aligned with your most dominant thoughts.

**"Your Life Moves Toward Your Most Dominate Thoughts."**

The Bible confirms this law. ***"For as he thinks in his heart, so is he…" (Proverbs 23:7 NKJV)*** Could it be, the life you are living today is in direct connection to the thoughts you had in your past? If you change your thinking, you can change your life. I believe this completely. I have heard it said that you are what you eat; but in reality, you are what you think.

**ATTRACTION IN ACTION**

This law is important. Why is it important? All of your faith and expectations are shaping up what you are thinking about, and in some strange mystical power, what we think creates what we feel. What we feel decides what we do, and what we do creates the motion to attract our future. This law attracts money, people and atmospheres. I read a book some time ago by Napoleon Hill, "***Think and Grow Rich***." I recommend this book for anyone who desires to be a millionaire. The whole theme of the book is ***if you think it and believe it, you can achieve it.*** This sounds biblical to me.

This "attraction" does not necessarily mean that money is attracted to you. It could mean that by having these positive thoughts that information is going to be revealed to you, maybe through books, mentors or even opportunities. Through the thoughts that you have, and the resulting actions that you take, the law of attraction will eventually bring into your life whatever it is that you are most focused on.

Use this law to attract more money into your life by focusing your attention on things that bring you closer to the achievement of your dreams. I am not advocating for you to ignore crisis or bad things that happen. What I am suggesting is that you do not allow them to consume your mind and take up the space for positive thinking.

5. ***The Law of Reflection:***

The law of reflection states that your outer world is a reflection of your inner world and corresponds with your dominant thoughts. This explains why most people become successful or unsuccessful, are happy or unhappy, or are wealthy or poor. Their world around them agrees to the world that exists in their inner thoughts. What is happening in you is deciding what is happening around you. Self-image is a major key to your success. ***You will never outperform your own self-image.***

**"Your Outer World Is A Reflection of Your Inner World."**

Ultimately, what this means when it comes to your financial situation is that nothing will change for you on the outside until it first changes for you in your mind. Everyone should aim to create a mental equivalent inside their mind of the things that they would like to experience in the outside world. Unless you create it in your mind first, it cannot be created around you.

**Process to Reflection:**
1. Revelation
2. Recognition
3. Relationship
4. Reflection

***Revelation*** is what everyone seems to be overly focused on. Everyone wants a revelation. Revelation simply means I can see. Revelation occurs when what has been blind to you is now revealed. However, seeing is not enough. Compassion sees, but we must grow and progress beyond seeing into being!

Revelation says I see. ***Recognition*** gives meaning to what I am seeing. Recognition says I appreciate what I see. I honor it. I am now identifying what I see as something more than revelation. It is now taking meaning and shape to me. For instance, I see God! That is a revelation. I do not just see; I see God! God is everywhere. There is more!

Revelation says I see. Recognition gives me clarity on what I am seeing. ***Relationship*** brings what I am seeing and moves it where it is connected to me. *I see... I see God.... I see God with me.* This, my friend, is where we begin to move into another dimension.

Revelation says I see. Recognition gives meaning to what I am seeing. Relationship brings what I am seeing and connects it to me. The real power is in Reflection. ***Reflection*** says I see what is in me. I John 4:4 says, *"Greater is He that is in me than He that is in the world."* Luke 17:21 says, *"The kingdom is neither here nor there, but the kingdom of God is* *within you..." (Paraphrased)* I see... I see God... I see God with me... I now see God in me! Wealth is attached to this level.

6. ***The Law of Lavishness:***
This law could also be called the law of abundance. The law of abundance states that we live in a lavish and bountiful universe in which there are plenty of blessings for all. There is enough wealth and resources for anyone who wants it; that is of course providing that you are willing to do what it takes to get it. This is more evident now in this century than any other time in history. There are more millionaires and billionaires than any other time.

When banks first started hundreds of years ago, they provided people with safety deposit boxes and a safe place to keep their gold coins, bars and money. Now, we are experiencing a different kind of wealth, digital wealth. Since we have entered the digital age, there has been an endless supply of money being pumped around the world every day. Money is not scarce. Money is everywhere. There isn't a lack of money; there is a lack of people having it. If you are willing to do what it takes to move into a different mindset, you can have a piece of this lavished resource that is waiting on you to take it. ***Action creates reward.*** We have all heard that *"good things come to those who wait. But great things come to those who do!" Kevin Mullens*

**"Good Things Come To Those Who Wait, But Great Things Come To Those Who Do!" Kevin Mullens**

7. ***The Law of sowing and reaping:***
The whole universe works on this law; the law of exchange. We are a medium to something bigger. This law states that money is a medium through which we exchange it for something else. We move it as we see its value in what it can do for us. You can spend money and live in the now. You can invest it, and live better in your future. I like the word invest, but in the Bible or church arena, you may hear it called sowing or giving. There is a fact in the Bible that few seem to really grasp. Luke 6:38 say, *"Give and it will be given back to you..."* What you have can turn into more! *"It comes back to you, increase and running over..." (paraphrased)* WOW! How can we miss this law! The law of exchange has been around before there was money. People would barter what they had for something they needed. Today, we use money. In times past, they used whatever they had - skill, seed, crops, etc.

We call it work! We work for a set amount of time and receive a set amount of money in return. Then we use the money that we have earned to buy goods or services from other people who are also exchanging their goods and services for money. This is sowing and reaping. In economics, this exchange is referred to as ***"real flows."*** Now it is said that this exists in a ***"circular flow"*** because the income of one individual equates to an expense of another. The Bible calls it sowing and reaping or the *law of reciprocity.*

**Value decides Rewards:**

Value is proportional to reward. The law of exchange dictates that the amount of money you receive for a product or service depends on how valuable it is. Value is decided by the more something is needed, the fewer people who have it and how important it is. The value will decide how much money that someone will exchange for it. This is referred to as ***Supply and Demand!*** This is extremely important for you to understand. When you are showing your business plan, you have to build into the listener's mind the reasons that they have to have it. Create value!

**"Money Is Influence. People Don't Follow Broke People."**

**Three Factors that determine value:**

1. The type of work you do (performance).
2. How well you do it (excellence).
3. The difficulty in finding what you do elsewhere (skill).

***8. The Law that Cash Is KING:***

This is the law of capital. What is your earning ability? The amount of money you earn today is a direct measure of the extent to which you have developed your earning ability. The higher your earning ability is, the more money you are going to have or make. ***Money is influence.*** Your ability to earn money and store money gives you a higher level of being heard by others. People do not follow broke people. Raise your level of learning; you will raise your level of earnings. Time is money. Time is what you have been given to trade off for anything else you want to have. Time wasters never have money and are always in need.

If you want to become wealthy and you desire to build a big business, you must be prepared to spend however long it takes to create something of high enough value that people want to buy into it.

**"Raise Your Level Of Learning; You Will Raise Your Level of Earnings."**

If time and money are spent learning new skills and knowledge, you will increase your personal value, which will then increase your future earning ability, and your money will grow. This is why you should always invest a portion of your income each month into personal development, so that you can work on becoming better. ***To build a bigger business, build a bigger you!***

9. ***The Law Of Saving:***
   The law of saving states that it is not how much money you make that will determine your financial future, but rather, how much of your money you are able to keep. Making a lot of money does not mean you are establishing a wealthy future. There are many people who make a lot of money over the course of there working life, but they retire broke and poor because they did not manage their money well and spent it needlessly.

**The Difference between the Rich and the Poor**

The financially successful are always concerned on cutting costs and saving money so that they can have more of it. The rich buy for assets and loss most of the time. The rich spend for profit. The poor spend for what they need. The rich spend on what they want. The poor buy what they do not want. You do not get what you deserve; you get what you are willing to negotiate for. The poor will always serve the rich (Proverb 22:7). The wealthy are experts at cutting costs and saving money for a rainy day.

Those who are not financially successful tend to do the exact opposite of those who are rich. They are experts at spending their money, but they have nothing left for the future. They live for today with little or no regard for their long-term financial future.

Wealth building occurs by accumulating as many assets as you can and reducing the number of financial obligations, or liabilities, that you have. This is called the power of compound interests.

***10. The Law Of Time and Timing:***

This law is the law of perspective. It states that the people who become most successful in life are those who look at things from a timing perspective and not time. Time is now; timing is later. We live in time, and our future exists in timing. What I do in time eventually is revealed in timing. We must become more eternally focused and not "now" focused. You will study and consider every decision when you do this; knowing a decision today has a tomorrow consequence attached to it. ***"Wrong decisions trigger the law of unintended consequences."***

One afternoon I received a phone call from my good friend and mentor, Dr. Mike Murdock. He said "Son, I have a revelation that is stunning." He then laid this on me. ***"Decisions decide wealth."*** Then he proceeded to tell me to place any word after the word "decide." Decisions decide health, relationships, consequences, anger, love…do you get it? Time and Timing!

When someone begins to think about things using this law of perspective, they generally do so because they have decided upon what they want to achieve and are willing to do whatever it takes to get it. They think about the consequences of their choices, and then decide whether following a particular course of action will help them reach their goal. As a result, most people who become financially successful in life have done so by being very careful with their decisions and how they spend money. They only spend it when it is absolutely necessary.

**"Wrong Decisions Trigger the Law of Unintended Consequences."**

***11. The Law of 80/20:***

This is the law of accelerating acceleration. This law states that 80% of your success will come from the last 20% of the time you put into something. This is amazing if you think about it because it means that you will achieve only about 20% of the total success possible for you in the first 80% of the time or money that you invest into something. What am I trying to tell you? Most millionaires do not become millionaires overnight, but rather, were able to achieve their wealth because of many years of consistent and focused effort.

Real wealth is built over time. It is often from a slow process, especially when you are first starting out. You will eventually begin to experience wealth and success if you stick with something for a long term. Again, we see that we cannot be in a hurry.

Take your time and learn when you set out to build your business. Grow your mind. Listen to your up line. Do not be impatient. Keep focused, persevere, endure, and you will succeed in any business.

***12. The Law of Eventuality*:**

If you keep doing what you are supposed to keep doing, you will eventually end up where you have set your sights. It is like taking a trip where you have to drive a long distance. Set your GPS, stay in the flow, do not deviate from your focus and you will eventually arrive to your destination. The key to this law is to know where to go. Know how to set the GPS and then engage. You have to leave the harbor if you want to experience the ocean. A ship is safer in the harbor, but ships were not built to stay in the harbor. They are built to sail the open seas. Yes, it is more dangerous, but it is also more exciting.

**"Ships Are Safer In The Harbor, But Ships Aren't Built For The Harbor, They're Built To Experience The Ocean"**

# CHAPTER ELEVEN

# EXCUSES KILL MOVEMENT

*"Excuses are the skin of reason, stuffed with a lie!" – Billy Sunday*

*"Never make excuses. Your friends don't need them and your foes won't believe them." — John Wooden,*

*"He that is good for making excuses is seldom good for anything else." — Benjamin Franklin*

There is a reason people stay broke, poor and miserable. It has never been God's will for anyone to live in ***poverty, pain or lack***. Anyone who believes otherwise has a bit of evil in them in my opinion. I believe every person has been given special gifting's to be something more than ***average*** in their life. There are too many 'middle of the road' people these days. "*Fence Riders*" is what I call them. People seem to be afraid to take a stand, choose a side and pick a leader. We are waiting to see what the majority is going to do. Leaders do not wait to see what others are doing; they do what they believe needs be done. They **LEAD**! There is a reason the majority are staying in the middle. The reason so many are stuck in the middle of their lives is that they are not willing to do what is necessary to move beyond the ordinary into the extraordinary.

***There is a big difference between being delivered and being free.***

Here's the truth...***wealth is not about money.*** *You can have money and not be wealthy, but you cannot be wealthy and not have money*! Wealthy people are about one thing, **FREEDOM!** I have already brought this up once. The middle class live month to month. The rich live year to year, but the wealthy live decade to decade. They are free! The middle class spends for a desired result. They are driven by what they want now. The rich spend for profit. They are always thinking about the profit that can be made on the things they invest in. There is a book titled, "The Millionaire Next Door." In that book, it references that most millionaires live in your neighborhood and not in rich neighborhoods. Why? They are more focused on what they have in balance than what they have in material. In other words, they like to see how much money they have accumulated verses how much they spend.

There is a difference from being delivered and being set free. Delivered means you no longer live in a certain place. You are no longer bound to a certain taskmaster. You are no longer living in a place where someone is consistently telling you what to do.

I believe all business people and entrepreneurs need to read and learn the story of the children of Israel in the book of Exodus. It is about how God delivered them from the hand of bondage and from the land of bondage into a Promised Land. You could say it this way, "From rags to riches."

God sent Moses to Egypt to lead His people, the Israelites, out of the land of bondage. God performed some incredible miracles to persuade Pharaoh to let them go and be free from bondage.

It is not enough to get you to leave a certain place, a certain lifestyle and a certain neighborhood. There are two phrases I want you to remember, the "hand of bondage" and "land of bondage." The hand is deliverance. The land is being set free. God brought them out of the hand of the enemy that had them, but that was not the enemy that would defeat them. Their greatest enemy was not someone but something. Their minds! Their thought life! They still thought of themselves as slaves!

**"The Middle Place Is the Testing Place For Movement"**

God moved these people from the hand of

bondage and began to take them into a ***NEW LAND***! God had to take them through something to get them to something. I hope you are starting to pick up the meaning of where I am taking you. The place God took them was the middle (wilderness). He brought them from captivity, into the wilderness, before He could take them to promise.

There is another word that we can use for wilderness and that word is transition. Transition is the place between two seasons, two places; between the season that was and the season that is. Transition is the hallway where one door has closed, but you are still waiting for the next door to open. Everything about your next door will be decided while you are in the hallway waiting for an open door. *That middle place is the testing place for movement.* Past the test and you will have the money. The word testimony means you have a story to tell about your test, your trial, your situation and your wilderness.

It was in that middle place or desert where God was attempting to free His people. They were delivered, and they were instantly blessed. They left their captivity with most of the wealth of Egypt. So you can be delivered and have blessings but still fail the test! Having blessings is not enough. Being moved from the place of bondage is not enough. You have to pass the test of the middle to be set **FREE**! Here is a verse that really brings chills to my spine...

*"Moreover, brethren, I do not want you to be unaware that all our fathers were under the cloud, all passed through the sea, all were baptized into Moses in the cloud and in the sea, all ate the same spiritual food, and all drank the same spiritual drink. For they drank of that spiritual Rock that followed them, and that Rock was*

*Christ.* ***But with most of them God was not well pleased, for their bodies were scattered in the wilderness. (*****The middle place*****)*** *Now these things became our examples..." (I Corinthians 10:1-6)*

WOW! If you believe this passage then you had better believe this. You can be delivered and never be set free. You can go to work and never have money. You can be married and never be happy. You can do, do, do, and never be satisfied. The reason is you have not changed the one necessary thing that needs to change. You have changed jobs. You have changed friends. You have changed your appearance. The thing you need to change is not around you but within you.

**"Until Your Mind Changes, Nothing Changes"**

***Your mind has to change.*** Your thinking has to change. The content of your life has to be richer and fuller than the container. Content is stronger than the container. The children of Israel were led out of bondage. God showed them who He was every day, but the problem was that God could not get them to rethink their lives.

Are you in this same scenario? There were reasons they were stuck in the middle. Freed from the hand but still mentally bound to the land. There are signs that prove you are still stuck in the middle (wilderness).

**Reason One: EXCUSES**

Excuses are the skin of reason stuffed with a lie. We have all made excuses for the reasons we have not changed. Excuses are anchors that keep you bound to failure and mediocrity. *"I'm too tired... I don't feel motivated... I'd rather not try right now... I have too much on my plate at this time... I don't have enough time... I don't have enough money... I can't because!"* **Excuses!** The number one reason to stay in the wilderness is excuses. No one will ever be a success as long as they can keep justifying their failures.

**"He That Is Good At Making Excuses Is Seldom Good For Anything Else"**
**Benjamin Franklin**

***Excuses are the nails used to build the house of failure.***

I love this quote: *"People spend too much time finding other people to blame, too much energy finding excuses for not being what they are capable of being, and not enough energy putting themselves on the line, growing out of the past, and getting on with their lives." J. Michael Straczynski*

Facts about excuses:

1. ***Excuses become the language of the unmotivated.*** People who have become lazy tend to make up so many reasons why they can't.
2. ***Excuses are the keys to procrastination.*** Procrastinators love to do everything tomorrow. Tomorrow <noun> *"A mystical land where 99% of all human productivity, motivation and achievement is stored."*
3. ***Excuses are the voice of the unchangeable, un-trainable and uninvolved.***

Moses had so many excuses when God begin to assign him a task. I believe these excuses live in us all and need to be dealt with in order to move out of lack and failure. (Exodus 3:1-12)

1. **The Excuse of Inability:** Moses responds to God when called, *"I'm a nobody and therefore unqualified to go and demand the release of the Lord's people."* This is a self-image problem. This is where we feel within ourselves powerless, incompetent and useless. You will never move to your dreams until you see yourself worthy and qualified to move forward.
2. **The Excuse of Inadequacy:** Again, this is a self-image problem. You will never rise above the person you think you are if you feel inadequate. Begin to do what you need to do to become equipped.
3. **The Excuse of Inferiority:** Once again, this is a self-image problem. What causes us to feel inferior? We cannot forget our past failures.
4. **The Excuse of Infirmity:** Here is where we begin to sell our weaknesses. We make excuses because we do not have the right size, stature, height and weight.

NO MORE:

NO MORE I'll do it tomorrow.
NO MORE buts.
NO MORE I can't.
NO MORE it's too hard.
NO MORE I'm too tired.
NO MORE waiting for it to get easier.
NO MORE putting it off.
NO MORE I don't have enough money.
NO MORE I'm not good enough… **NO MORE EXCUSES!**

**Reason Two: Stubbornness and Rebellion**
Stubborn people will never change. You cannot help anyone who is stubborn.

***Stubbornness....*** unreasonably hard to move, inflexible, wrong thinking, and headstrong. The definition I like the most is someone who will not change one's attitude, opinion or position on something- especially in spite of a good argument or reason to do so. How can anyone move out of their wilderness with a stubborn attitude?

There is a big difference between being stubborn and being determined. Determined means I have decided on a desired result, but I still am in the mindset to learn on the way. A stubborn mind does not want to hear anything. Stubborn people know they should, but will not. They refuse to listen for change. They have decided to not cut off pleasure for the sake of change and truth.

> **"I do not think much of a man who is not wiser today than he was yesterday."**
> **Abraham Lincoln**

*"Those who never retract their opinions love themselves more than they love truth." — Joseph Joubert*

**Facts about Stubbornness**

1. *Stubbornness causes God to turn you over to your own desires.*
2. *Stubbornness will cause you to always move backwards (Jeremiah 7:24).*
3. *Stubbornness will unlock the curse, not the covenant.*
4. *Stubbornness makes you useless to God.*

5. *Stubbornness removes protection over your life.*
6. *Stubbornness stores up God's wrath.*

**Signs of Stubbornness:**

1. An angry mind and spirit.
2. A refusal to change.
3. An attitude that keeps you from knowing what is right.
4. An unwillingness to hear the truth.
5. An unwillingness to face your past.
6. A refusal to cut off old ways and ideas.

Here's the difference between being determined verses being stubborn minded.

1. ***Determined people are not easily persuaded but are willing to change. Stubborn people are not willing to change.***
2. ***Determined people know what they want and what they do not want.***
3. ***Determined people pave their own paths.***
4. ***Determined people do not have a closed mind; they have a mind of their own.***

**Cure for stubbornness:**

1. A change of mind.
2. A change of methods.
3. A change of heart and motive.

# CHAPTER TWELVE

# WEAPONS THAT WILL STOP ABUNDANCE

*Every dreamer has an enemy. Every visionary has obstacles. Every type of advancement has opposition. Every desire has limitations.*

You must understand that sometimes you are going to come up short in your life. You are going to have to face warfare and battle to fulfill your dreams, visions and plans. Enemies are not always bad. On the contrary, ***enemies are necessary***. You would not know that what you are attempting to do is worth doing without opposition. ***Enemies decide rewards.*** An enemy gives your vision the power to be real. Enemies create the reality that your dream is worth fighting for. I can tell you this through my experience that whenever I have attempted anything worth doing, opposition showed up immediately. That opposition was sometimes as small as just someone saying they did not believe what I was doing or attempting to do was going to work. You need to know the weapons that an enemy will use to bring your dreams and vision to failure.

**"Enemies Are Necessary"**
**"Enemies Decide Rewards"**

**WEAPON NUMBER ONE is *DISTRACTION*:**

An enemy will use this weapon in so many inconspicuous ways. It is used in conversation. It is used in noise. It can happen through crisis and situations. Something will happen to attempt to take you off course. It could be as simple as a fight with your spouse; your children not doing what they are supposed to do. It can happen through breakdowns and equipment failure. Everything can be going great and all of a sudden a tire goes flat, someone hits your car from behind, a check bounces, someone steals your identity.

My wife and I were spending a week in Fort Lauderdale, Florida for the international yacht and boat show. While we were in Florida, attempting to relax and enjoy ourselves, I received an email that my credit score had taken a drastic dive. I am very focused on keeping up with my credit score. I begin to research and when I got to the bottom of it, I was the victim of identity theft. I was so angry, frustrated and felt very much violated. It was about to ruin my whole day. Then I changed perspective. This was an attempt to distract me from enjoying my wife and a day with her. I decided not to let my situation decide my day. I will decide my day regardless of the situation.

Men always fail in broken focus. The enemy is after your focus. If you break your focus, you will stop seeing what you were about to possess. Just about the time that you are to possess your increase, expect the enemy of distraction to show up. Never allow your situation to define you. You define your situation! God has given you what you need to overcome them.

**WEAPON NUMBER TWO is IMPATIENCE:**

Impatience can be costly. Research suggests that people who opt for smaller rewards today over bigger rewards later tend to have lower credit scores. In a study by Columbia Business School associate professor Stephan Meier, the most impatient people have credit scores below 620, which mean they pay more for loans.

An experiment published in the June 2011 edition of the Journal of Consumer Research found that consumers make money choices based on how connected they feel to their future identities. In that experiment, the researchers asked graduating seniors at the University of Chicago to read one of two statements: The first emphasized the enormity of graduating college and how much they would change afterward. The second one did just the reverse. It emphasized that their core identity changes little throughout the course of their life. Then participants were told that they could receive a gift card right away or a bigger gift card later.

**"Impatience Is Costly"**

The results were clear. Students who read the statement that focused on change were more likely to opt for the lower-valued gift card (worth $120) immediately. Those who read the statement emphasizing continuity in their identity were more likely to elect to receive the larger gift card later (worth up to $240).

That study goes back to an even earlier, classic experiment most famous for its use of marshmallows. Back in the 1970s, Stanford University researchers offered children a choice, one marshmallow now or two later. Based on follow-up studies, the children who opted for two treats later were more likely to be successful in life, suggesting that the ability to defer gratification is a valuable trait.

The recurring theme in these studies is that patience is a powerful gift for succeeding. Delayed gratification is trained. You are not born to understand delayed rewards; you are taught it. The number one reason people struggle with money is their parents never taught them about money.

The more you connect to your future, the more you will be able to be patient and wait on your future's arrival.

**EIGHT STEPS TO FINANCIAL RECOVERY:**

1. Identify the bigger picture.
2. Do some introspection.
3. Monitor your credit score.
4. Boost your credit score slowly.
5. Seek financial mentors.
6. Study your spending patterns daily.
7. Give yourself an allowance.
8. Be focused to stay on track.

**FIVE MONEY SAVING EXERCISES:**

Think of your money as if it is your body. The more physically fit you are has major benefits for being proactive in your life. The same can be said about your money. Financial fitness is the product of a continual process. Just as your body does not change overnight, the same is true about your financial fitness.

1. ***Review Your Account Statement Diligently For Errors.*** Do not rush through your financial bank statement. Take time to balance your books monthly. You have to know where you are leaking money.
2. ***Never Miss A Due Date On Your Bills.*** Failing to pay on time is perhaps the easiest (and most avoidable) way to damage your credit score. If you are not very good at remembering to pay your bills, set up automatic monthly payments.
3. ***Be Focused On Your Physical Health.*** Being unhealthy can become very costly. Take the time

to manage your eating habits and exercise. Look at it as an investment in saving you money in the long run.

4. ***Be Proactive In Protecting Your Identity.*** I can tell you first hand that "Identity Theft" can be stressful and costly.
5. ***Invest In Yourself.*** Setting aside a portion of each paycheck is the wisest thing you will ever do. You are important! You are worth the investment. Remember, the story of the one marshmallow now or two marshmallows later.

Financial management is all about being realistic. You need to be ***"Growth Minded"*** and believe in the promise of the future in order to be able to set long-term goals. Overcome the desire to gratify yourself now and work the power of compound. [9]

**REASONS WHY YOU'RE NOT BEING PROMOTED:**

1. ***Cheating your day:*** You are supposed to work. There is no getting around it. No work, no reward. People cheat themselves every day. They waste more time than they are productive.
2. ***Wrong appearances:*** People see you before they hear you. The way you dress can be costing you dearly. Watch television and read Forbes magazine; notice how the successful dress. Make sure you have not hurt yourself by your appearance. If you are not sure about it, ask

[9] Footnote U.S. News and World Report/Money money.usnews.com/money/blogs/my-money/2015/12/03/5-money-saving-exercises-to-achieve-financial-fitness interest.

someone. Like it or not, image matters! You are not on vacation. The easiest thing to do when you work for yourself is begin to become lazy in your appearance.

3. ***No intensity in what you do:*** Make sure you have urgency about your day. High achievers have intensity about what they are attempting to accomplish. Look alive! Passion is contagious.
4. ***You lack the relationship skills:*** No one succeeds alone. You are going to have to work on your connection and communication skills. You need to listen as well as you speak to be great at communicating.
5. ***You have no expectation:*** A life that has no expectation in it is no life at all. You will never be promoted in anything if you have no expectation.
6. ***You are not seeing the bigger picture.***

## *MAY I INVITE YOU TO MAKE JESUS CHRIST LORD OF YOUR LIFE?*

*The Bible says, **"That if you will confess with your mouth the Lord Jesus, and will believe in your heart that God raised Him from the dead, you will be saved. For with the heart man believes unto righteousness; and with the mouth confession is made for salvation."*** Romans 10:9, 10

**PRAY THIS PRAYER WITH ME TODAY:**

"Dear Jesus, I believe that You died for me, and that You rose again on the third day. I confess to You that I am a sinner. I need Your love and forgiveness. Come into my life, forgive my sins, and give me eternal life. I confess You now as my Lord and Savior. Thank You for my salvation! I walk in Your peace and joy from this day forward. Amen!"

Signed______________________________ Date _______

☐ Yes, I would like to be on your mailing list.

Name____________________________________________

Address__________________________________________

City___________________State _____ Zip___________

Phone:__________________Email:___________________

**Dr. Jerry A. Grillo, Jr**
P.O. Box 3707, Hickory N.C. 28603
1.888.328.6763 Fax: 828.325.4877
WWW.DRJERRYGRILLO.COM

## *WHAT OTHERS ARE SAYING*

Dr. Jerry Grillo lives what he teaches. It has been my privilege to be his personal friend for a number of years. He is a living example of a victorious leader. His church is a victorious church. If you can't succeed under this man of God, you can't succeed anywhere. His revelation is life's fresh air in a stagnant world. He is one of the happiest and most exciting leaders I have known through my thirty-eight years of world evangelism. It is my privilege to recommend any book he has written.

Dr. Mike Murdock
The Wisdom Center
Dallas, TX

Dr. Jerry Grillo is truly a gift from God to my life. I love his passion, his purity and his painstaking commitment to purpose. It is very obvious that he loves the God he preaches to us about. Should you ever have the privilege of speaking into this life, you would know without a doubt he's one of God's favorites. Bishop Grillo, what a wonderful refreshing, what a wonderful friend!

Sheryl Brady
Sheryl Brady Ministries

Bishop Grillo is fast becoming a leading voice of authority... Having him minister at our Emotional Healing Conference became a valuable training session to our leadership and a needed breakthrough to many of our members. To say that Bishop Grillo is qualified to pen these pages would be an understatement. You hold in your hand a key to unlocking the life that God desires for you. I dare you to turn these pages with even the least little bit of expectation and watch as God begins to show out in your life!

Bishop Jeff Poole
New Hope International
Warner Robins, GA

## TO INVITE DR. JERRY GRILLO TO SPEAK AT YOUR NEXT CONFERENCE, BUSINESS MEETING OR TO SCHEDULE TELEVISION OR RADIO INTERVIEWS

WRITE TO:

FOGZONE MINISTRIES
P.O. BOX 3707
HICKORY, NC. 28603
OR EMAIL: FZM@FOGZONE.NET
FAX INVITATION TO 828-325-4877
OR CALL 1-888 FAVOR ME

WWW.DRJERRYGRILLO.COM

**FOLLOW ME ON**

@BishopGrillo

@BishopGrillo

@BishopGrillo

@Godstrongtv

Made in the USA
Monee, IL
10 February 2022

90344686R00083